ANGELS AND DEMONS

BENNY HINN

ISBN: 978-0-9846515-0-4

Published by

LIFEBRIDGE
BOOKS
P.O. Box 49428
Charlotte, NC 28277
www.LifeBridgeBooks.com

Printed in the United States of America

CONTENTS

INTRODUCTION

The battle between right and wrong, moral and immoral, virtuous and vile is as old as recorded history. In the Garden of Eden God placed the Tree of the Knowledge of Good and Evil and directed man not to eat of it, adding that death would occur if man ate of that tree (Genesis 2:17). Man was given a choice whether to obey or disobey.

Today, the conflict still rages.

At times, good and evil can reside in the same person. Robert Louis Stevenson wrote about this in his famous book, *The Strange Case of Dr. Jekyll and Mr. Hyde*, the story of a man with a multiple personality disorder.

This internal fight is nothing new. The apostle Paul wrote about it more than 2,000 years ago when he said, *"For I know that in me (that is, in my flesh,) dwelleth no good thing: for to will is present with me; but how to perform that which is good I find not. For the good that I would I do not: but the evil which I would not, that I do"* (Romans 7:18-19).

In this book, you will come face to face with the two most opposing forces operating in our world: angels and demons. These are not figments of our imagination, but are real and active at this very moment.

As a minister of the Gospel, I have to battle the forces of Satan continually. They rear their ugly heads in our crusades and attempt to destroy what God is doing in hearts and lives around the world. Yet I can assure you from firsthand experience that the Almighty has sent His angels to protect and minister to me—more times than I can count.

Billy Graham once said, "Christians should never fail to sense the operation of an angelic glory. It forever eclipses the world of demonic powers, as the sun does a candle's light." I can testify that this is true.

I am excited that you have chosen to read this book. The study of angels and demons has been life-changing for me.

I pray that your life will be transformed as you understand what is taking place in the spirit world and discover who you are in Christ and the authority you have.

Let's begin.

– Benny Hinn

PART I

ANGELS

CHAPTER 1

GOD'S AMAZING ANGELIC BEINGS

Today, in our Western culture, the subject of angels is not only popular but well accepted. I'm sure someone at one time or another has told you, "I have a guardian angel watching over me."

If you try a Google search for *angels* on the Internet, you will find over 32 million entries. There is increasing curiosity, but most of the information is not biblical. In fact, in both the secular world and the church, there is great ignorance concerning the true nature and function of angels.

I am convinced there is just one place to look for the real answers—God's Word. It is the only reliable source of spiritual truth and accurate information pertaining to angels and angelic hosts. The pages of the Bible make reference to *angel* or *angels* approximately three hundred times. Also note that there are more references to angels in the Bible than there are to demons.

The English word *angel* is derived from the Hebrew word *mal`ak* and from the Greek word *angelos,* which both mean "messenger."

Angels belong to an order of heavenly beings who are superior to man in both power and intelligence. As the psalmist writes, "*What is man, that thou art mindful of him? and the son of man, that thou visitest him? For thou hast made him a little lower than the angels, and hast crowned him with glory and honour*" (Psalm 8:4-5).

The fact that man's order is lower than angels is repeated in Hebrews 2:7.

If we accept Scripture, we must also believe that angelic beings are real and that they minister to you and me—the "heirs of salvation." In addition, we must embrace the truth that although the spirit realm is invisible to the natural eye, it is as real as the physical world we live in. Angels are spiritual beings who exist in the spiritual realm, but God often sends them to earth to accomplish His will, to send a message, or to protect or deliver His people. As believers, one of our great privileges is the opportunity to receive help from God's special messengers.

LIFE-CHANGING ENCOUNTERS

From Genesis to Revelation, we find accounts of angels visiting people, intervening in their circumstances, advising, informing, and assisting them in countless ways. The Bible records over one hundred appearances of angels specifically sent from heaven to help direct the lives of people.

For example, it was an angel that appeared to Phillip and instructed him to go down the road toward Gaza to meet the Ethiopian eunuch (Acts 8).

In addition to the angels' ministry on earth, they are constantly at work in heaven, praising and worshiping the Almighty.

Most people find it easier to visualize angels in the heavenlies than to accept the fact that they also visit and assist us on earth. However, Christian history is replete with marvelous accounts of individuals who have had life-changing encounters with angels.

I believe we are about to enter into a season of supernatural manifestations as never seen before on this planet, and with every visitation comes angelic appearances. If you look back to the days of Abraham, when God visited the earth, you will find that angels were always present at those times. And we will see this phenomena happening again and again.

It is vital that we know what the Bible teaches concerning visitations from the spirit world, so we can be wise and discern whether or not they are sent from God.

SEVEN FACTS CONCERNING ANGELS

In this book we will turn to the pages of God's Word and unlock hidden truths pertaining to both angels and demons. As we begin, however, I want to lay a foundation concerning angelic beings. There are seven specific facts we need to know:

1. Angels were created by God before this planet came into existence.

Let me call your attention to an important passage of Scripture found in the book of Job. God is asking, *"Where wast thou when I laid the foundations of the earth? Declare, if thou hast understanding. Who hath laid the measures thereof,*

if thou knowest? Or who hath stretched the line upon it?" (Job
34:4-5). Then the Almighty continues, *"Whereupon are the
foundations thereof fastened? Or who laid the corner stone
thereof; when the morning stars sang together, and all the sons
of God shouted for joy?"* (verses 5-6).

There can be no other explanation than *"the sons of God"*
are angels. Why? Because this speaks of a time before the
earth was created. So these could not be human beings. In
addition, the word for God in this portion of Scripture is
Elohim. As humans, we were never called "sons of *Elohim*,"
rather "sons of *Jehovah*."

As further proof that angels were brought into being by
the Lord, the psalmist writes, *"Praise ye him, all his angels:
praise ye him, all his hosts. Praise ye him, sun and moon:
praise ye him, all ye stars of light. Praise him, ye heavens of
heavens, and ye waters that be above the heavens. Let them
praise the name of the LORD; for he commanded, and they
were created"* (Psalm 148:2-5).

Angels being part of creation is confirmed in the New
Testament as the apostle Paul tells us, *"For by him were all
things created, that are in heaven, and that are in the earth,
visible and invisible, whether they be thrones, or dominions,
or principalities, or powers: all things were created by him,
and for him"* (Colossians 1:16).

2. Angels are not to be worshiped.

We are commanded in Scripture, *"Let no man, therefore
judge you in meat, or in drink, or in respect of an holyday, or
the new moon, or of the sabbath days: which are a shadow
of things to come; but the body is of Christ. Let no man
beguile you of your reward in a voluntary humility and*

worshipping of angels" (Colossians 2:16-18).

When John had his great revelation, he made this statement: *"I fell down to worship before the feet of the angel which shewed me these things"* (Revelation 22:6). But the angel was quick to tell John, *"See thou do it not: for I am thy fellowservant, and of thy brethren the prophets, and of them which keep the sayings of this book: worship God* (verse 9).

Even though angels were God-formed and have specific purposes, we are not to pray to them, only to the Creator of both heaven and earth.

3. Angels are organized into principalities and powers.

Later we will discuss the five divisions of angels and their functions. We will also learn that there is more than one type of angelic host, but remember, *"whether... principalities, or powers: all things were created by him, and for him"* (Colossians 1:16). In certain instances they appear and operate as an organized army.

4. Angels are without number.

The Bible tells us, *"But ye are come unto mount Sion, and unto the city of the living God, the heavenly Jerusalem, and to an innumerable company of angels"* (Hebrews 12:22).

In the words of the prophet Jeremiah, *"As the host of heaven cannot be numbered, neither the sand of the sea measured: so will I multiply the seed of David my servant, and the Levites that minister unto me"* (Jeremiah 33:22).

When Jesus was on the cross He said He could have called *"twelve legions of angels"* to come to His aid (Matthew 26:53). A legion at that time referred to a Roman contingent of troops that numbered about 6,000. Twelve legions would be 72,000 angels!

To reinforce this point, John saw and heard *"the voice of many angels round about the throne and the beasts and the elders: and the number of them was ten thousand times ten thousand, and thousands of thousands"* (Revelation 5:11). They were praising with a loud voice, *"Worthy is the Lamb that was slain"* (verse 12).

What a choir that must have been!

5. Angels dwell in heaven and stand before God continually.

While it is true that angels visit the earth, they are permanent residents of heaven. Scripture records, *"Again he said, Therefore hear the word of the LORD; I saw the LORD sitting upon his throne, and all the host of heaven standing on his right hand and on his left"* (2 Chronicles 18:18).

They never stop worshiping the Creator. In the words of God's Son, *"Take heed that ye despise not one of these little ones; for I say unto you, that in heaven their angels do always behold the face of my Father which is in heaven"* (Matthew 18:10).

6. The majority of angels have the appearance of men.

As far back as Abraham, angels have appeared on earth in the form of men. As Abraham sat in the door of his tent one hot day on the plains of Mamre, he looked up and *"lo, three men stood by him: and when he saw them, he ran to meet them from the tent door, and bowed himself toward the ground, and said, My Lord, if now I have found favour in thy sight, pass not away, I pray thee, from thy servant: Let a little water, I pray you, be fetched, and wash your feet, and rest yourselves under the tree"* (Genesis 18:2-4).

Without question, these men were angels sent by God.

Later, in Joshua's day, an angel appeared to him as a soldier.

While Joshua was near Jericho, he looked up and standing right in front of him was *"a man over against him with his sword drawn in his hand"* (Joshua 5:13).

The prophet asked him, "Whose side are you on? Ours or the enemy's?"

The man told Joshua he wasn't on either side, *"but as captain of the host of the LORD am I now come"* (verse 14). Immediately, Joshua fell down and worshiped the angel and wanted to know, "What word do you have for me?

The angel told him to take off his shoes because he was standing on holy ground (verse 15). The prophet praised God and obeyed.

In the New Testament, just after the Resurrection, the angel seen by the women at the tomb was in the form of a *young* man. *"And entering into the sepulchre, they saw a young man sitting on the right side, clothed in a long white garment; and they were affrighted"* (Mark 16:5).

We also find angels appearing as earthly men at the time Jesus ascended back to the Father. As the apostles *"looked steadfastly toward heaven as he went up, behold, two men stood by them in white apparel; which also said, Ye men of Galilee, why stand ye gazing up into heaven? This same Jesus, which is taken up from you into heaven, shall so come in like manner as ye have seen him go into heaven"* (Acts 1:10-11).

These *"two men"* were God's messengers—angels—and

they had the appearance of normal men on earth.

7. Angels wear clothing.

How were the angels we just mentioned dressed? They wore *"white apparel"* (Acts 1:10). We find the same description after the Resurrection when Mary stood at the tomb weeping. As she grieved for her Son, she stooped down and looked into the sepulcher. There she saw *"two angels in white sitting, the one at the head, and the other at the feet, where the body of Jesus had lain"* (John 20:12).

THE UNSEEN WORLD

The "invisible" things of the heavenly world spoken of in Scripture are as real and understandable as the visible things seen on earth today. The apostle Paul spoke of Jesus being *"the image of the invisible God, the firstborn of every creature"* (Colossians 1:15). It is by Christ that *"all things [were] created, that are in heaven, and that are in earth, visible and invisible"* (verse 16).

"Invisible" doesn't mean it cannot be seen somewhere. It's only blocked from our vision because we are limited to this planet, but it is visible in a different realm. However, the line between the two is very thin. There is an invisible world in heaven, on earth, and under the earth. To you and me, however, we only see what is around us. Yet this does not mean that what is beyond our present isn't real. It exists, but in a different realm or location. We are housed in a body of flesh, but there are spirits in the world today we cannot see with our natural eyes. God created all things, *"and without him was not any thing made that was made"* (John 1:3).

16

As we will discuss later, not all of the dominions, principalities, and powers spoken of in Colossians 1 are holy. According to Ephesians 6:12, we are wrestling against evil beings, principalities, and diabolical dominions. However, the truth I want to emphasize is that all things were originally created holy and perfect.

God Almighty designed the visible world to give us evidence of the invisible world, not the other way around. The Creator, who is invisible, existed before there was an earth, before anything material. Angels, Satan, and demon spirits predate humanity. First came the spiritual, then the physical.

EVIDENCE THAT CAN'T BE IGNORED

Mankind may attempt to ignore the existence of God, but their reasoning is futile.

The apostle Paul makes this powerful argument: *"For the invisible things of him from the creation of the world are clearly seen, being understood by the things that are made, even his eternal power and Godhead; so that they are without excuse"* (Romans 1:20).

The glory of God and His invisible, eternal power is revealed through the visible world which He formed. So when you admire majestic mountains, exquisite flowers, or watch a man or woman walking down a path enjoying God's handiwork, it is evidence of a power that made it all possible—a divine force we cannot see.

Scripture tells us something quite remarkable: *"There are also celestial bodies, and bodies terrestrial: but the glory of the celestial is one, and the glory of the terrestrial is another"* (1 Corinthians 15:40). This speaks of an enormous universe that is unseen by humanity—the celestial (invisible) and the earthly (visible).

AN INSIGHT INTO THE HEAVENLIES

As we continue, we are going to look beyond the veil and see what the Bible has to say concerning what is now concealed. We are not searching for what is unattainable, so out of our reach we can never touch it, but are searching for a better place. That is what the heroes of faith sought. The writer of Hebrews referred to those who *"died in the faith, not having received the promises, but having seen them afar off, and were persuaded of them, and embraced them, and confessed that they were strangers and pilgrims on the earth"* (Hebrews 11:13).

What were they searching after? *"For they that say such things declare plainly that they seek a country. And truly, if they had been mindful of that country from whence they came out, they might have had opportunity to have returned. But now they desire a better country, that is, an heavenly: wherefore God is not ashamed to be called their God: for he hath prepared for them a city"* (verses 14-16).

They were looking for higher ground, the invisible kingdom of God. Even though they couldn't see it, they knew it was there. The Bible states in Isaiah, *"for my thoughts are not your thoughts, neither are your ways my ways, saith the* LORD. *For as the heavens are higher than the earth, so are my ways higher than your ways, and my thoughts than your thoughts"* (Isaiah 55:8-9).

The Holy Bible is the only book ever written that gives us an insight into the heavenlies and allows us to peek into what lies beyond. There are literally hundreds of Scriptures revealing all we need to know about this unseen world. We often miss the truth because we become bogged down in so many details, but what is spoken of is tangible and real. We are called to sit in heavenly places.

I pray that as we delve into the amazing revelations concerning both angels and demons, your heart, soul, and mind will hear from heaven. God is waiting to unlock His treasure-trove of knowledge just for you.

WHAT ABOUT "EVIL" ANGELS?

If you think all angels are good and obey God's voice, think again! We know from Isaiah 14:12-13, that angels can make choices, as did Lucifer, who we will discuss in Chapter 5.

However, the Almighty knows which angels disobey Him, and there will be a severe price to pay. Scripture tells us that *"the angels which kept not their first estate, but left their own habitation, he hath reserved in everlasting chains under darkness unto the judgment of the great day"* (Jude 6).

In certain instances (like dealing with Egypt during the time of Moses), God sends "evil angels" to do His work. As the psalmist wrote, *"He cast upon them the fierceness of his anger, wrath, and indignation, and trouble, by sending evil angels among them"* (Psalm 78:49).

In the final analysis, there is no hope for disobedient angels. They are doomed to spend eternity in the lake of fire. "Then shall he say also unto them on the left hand, Depart from me, ye cursed, into everlasting fire, prepared for the devil and his angels" (Matthew 25:41).

As a believer, you cannot be torn away from your heavenly Father even by evil angels. You can say with Paul,

"For I am persuaded, that neither death, nor life, nor angels, nor principalities, nor powers, nor things present, nor things to come, nor height, nor depth, nor any other creature, shall be able to separate us from the love of God, which is in Christ Jesus our Lord" (Romans 8:38-39).

I like what Martin Luther, the leader of the Reformation, once said: "Let your holy Angel have charge concerning us, that the wicked one have no power over us."

Amen!

CHAPTER 2

THE SIX-WINGED
SERAPHIM

W hen most people think of an angel, they have a
mental image of a celestial being with wings—resembling an
ornament hanging on a Christmas tree. Or a cherub with a
bow and arrow adorning a Valentine's Day card.

As we open the pages of God's Word, however, we
discover more than one type of angel. They appear in unique
forms, at different times, for specific purposes. In fact, there
are five separate divisions of angels mentioned in the Bible:
seraphim, cherubim, archangels, living creatures, and
common angels. Let's look at the first division called the
seraphim.

WHAT IS THEIR FUNCTION?

This is one category of the angelic host we know very little
about. Who are the seraphim? What is their function?

The seraph, or the seraphim, are mentioned just twice in
the Bible—and only in one portion of Scripture. The

prophet Isaiah writes, *"In the year that king Uzziah died I saw also the LORD sitting upon a throne, high and lifted up, and his train [the skirt of His robe] filled the temple. Above it stood the seraphims: each one had six wings; with twain he covered his face, and with twain he covered his feet, and with twain he did fly"* (Isaiah 6:1-2).

What an amazing description. Try to visualize one of these angels with six wings—two hiding his face (he could not look at God's glory), two covering his feet (recognizing subservience to the Almighty), and two for flying (taking care of God's business). The fact they are called seraphim (plural) means there are many of them. We aren't given an exact number, but we do know they stand over the throne of God.

"HOLY, HOLY, HOLY"

There is no record as to where seraphim fly, but they have never been seen on earth. Perhaps this is what Paul was referring to when he talked about being caught up to the third heaven and witnessing things he could not explain (2 Corinthians 12:2-4).

We read, *"One [seraph] cried unto another, and said, Holy, holy, holy, is the LORD of hosts: the whole earth is full of his glory"* (Isaiah 6:3).

Their function as described here is to speak to each other about God's holiness and His great acts. These angels in heaven, with wings covering their eyes, continually cry out and worship the Almighty. The result of their speaking is a tremendous release of God's presence. *"And the posts of the door moved at the voice of him that cried, and the house was filled with smoke"* (verse 4). This was a commotion so great that it shook the very foundation of the temple in heaven where God abides. The doors began to vibrate!

When Isaiah witnessed this awesome event, he was so frightened that he exclaimed, *"Woe is me! for I am undone; because I am a man of unclean lips, and I dwell in the midst of a people of unclean lips: for mine eyes have seen the King, the LORD of hosts"* (verse 5).

Next, we learn that one of the seraphim, *"having a live coal in his hand, which he had taken with the tongs from off the altar...laid it upon my mouth, and said, Lo, this hath touched thy lips; and thine iniquity is taken away, and thy sin purged"* (Isaiah 6:6-7).

This opens our eyes to something else about these angels. In addition to their wings, they have hands. When the prophet's lips were touched by the angel, his iniquity was removed. However, since angels do not have the authority to forgive sin, the seraph was speaking on God's behalf.

CHAPTER 3

THE FOUR-FACED CHERUBIM

Seraphim were seen by Isaiah, but cherubim were witnessed by the prophet Ezekiel.

It was the cherubim that protected the Tree of Life from Adam and Eve after the Creator banished them from the Garden of Eden because of their sin. *"Therefore the LORD God sent him forth from the garden of Eden, to till the ground from whence he was taken. So he drove out the man; and he placed at the east of the garden of Eden Cherubims, and a flaming sword which turned every way, to keep the way of the tree of life"* (Genesis 3:23-25)

Scripture tells us much more about these heavenly hosts. Centuries later, after Ezekiel had a vision of God, he began to see these particular angels. He wrote, *"Then I looked, and, behold, in the firmament that was above the head of the cherubims there appeared over them as it were a sapphire stone, as the appearance of the likeness of a throne"* (Ezekiel 10:1).

Verse 21 of this same chapter gives this description: *"Every one had four faces apiece, and every one four wings;*

25

and the likeness of the hands of a man was under their wings."

That is most revealing. Seraphim have six wings while cherubim have only four, but the most unusual aspect is that each has four faces.

OUT OF A WHIRLWIND

To discover what was taking place, it's important to refer back to the first chapter of Ezekiel:

> *Now it came to pass in the thirtieth year, in the fourth month, in the fifth day of the month, as I was among the captives by the river of Chebar, that the heavens were opened, and I saw visions of God. In the fifth day of the month, which was the fifth year of king Jehoiachin's captivity, the word of the LORD came expressly unto Ezekiel the priest, the son of Buzi, in the land of the Chaldeans by the river Chebar; and the hand of the LORD was there upon him.*
>
> *And I looked, and, behold, a whirlwind came out of the north, a great cloud, and a fire infolding itself, and a brightness was about it, and out of the midst thereof as the colour of amber, out of the midst of the fire* (Ezekiel 1:1-4).

From the north there approached what looked like a tornado. Wrapped in this whirlwind was a cloud and fire, and it was headed straight towards the prophet. What happened next was startling: *"Also out of the midst thereof came the likeness of four living creatures. And this was their appearance; they had the likeness of a man. And every one had four faces, and every one had four wings"* (Ezekiel 1:5-6).

Notice, Ezekiel 10 refers to them as cherubim, but Ezekiel 1 calls them living creatures. But they are the same, each with four faces and four wings. *"Their feet were straight feet; and the sole of their feet was like the sole of a calf's foot: and they sparkled like the colour of burnished brass"* (Ezekiel 1:7). These creatures were gleaming!

In addition, *"they had the hands of a man under their wings"* (verse 8; see also Ezekiel 10). And we learn that the wings of the cherubim *"were joined one to another; they turned not when they went; they went every one straight forward"* (Ezekiel 1:9).

They undertook their assigned duties in total unity.

THE FOUR FACES

For a moment, picture a row of angels bound to each other unable to be separated.

Where one goes, they all go. Remember, they had never been seen by man with the exception of Adam, when the cherubim protected the Tree of Life. They were probably surrounding the tree since there was more than one of these angels.

In Ezekiel's vision, the line of four-faced cherubim were walking forward together. What were the four faces? Scripture tells us they had *"the face of a man, and the face of a lion, on the right side: and they four had the face of an ox on the left side; they four also had the face of an eagle"* (Ezekiel 1:10).

I want to add here an important truth about this portion of scripture. The mention of the four faces of the cherubs is also a revelation of the Lord Jesus. The face of a man speaks of His humanity; the face of the lion speaks of His authority; the face of the ox speaks of His sacrifice on the cross; and the face of the eagle speaks of His deity.

This is amazing, but there's still more. We learn that *"their wings were stretched upward; two wings of every one were joined one to another, and two covered their bodies"* (verse 11).

I can visualize these angels with the face of a man, a lion, an ox, and an eagle, all marching in unison, with their upper wings joining them together. With their second set of wings they covered their bodies. The Bible adds this important point: *"Whither the spirit was to go, they went; and they turned not when they went"* (verse 12). In other words, the cherubim always follow the Holy Spirit.

LIKE LIGHTNING!

Their description of there living creatures defies imagination. *"Their appearance was like burning coals of fire, and like the appearance of lamps: it went up and down among the living creatures; and the fire was bright, and out of the fire went forth lightning. And the living creatures ran and returned as the appearance of a flash of lightning"* (verses 13-14).

Even though the cherubim were united as if tied together, they moved back and forth with incredible speed as one!

Earlier, we discovered the seraphim was dressed in white, but not the cherubim. They appeared like red-hot burning fire!

WHEELS WITHIN WHEELS

In verse 20 we are told once more that theirs was a Spirit-guided mission. *"Whithersoever the spirit was to go, they went, thither was their spirit to go; and the wheels were lifted up over against them: for the spirit of the living creature was in the wheels."*

I've heard some people speculate that these "wheels" mentioned here were flying saucers. That's foolishness. The cherubim were *riding* on wheels of fire!

As Ezekiel looked at these living creatures, *"behold one wheel upon the earth by the living creatures, with his four faces. The appearance of the wheels and their work was like unto the colour of a beryl: and they four had one likeness: and their appearance and their work was as it were a wheel in the middle of a wheel"* (Ezekiel 1:15-16).

There were two wheels—one outer, one inner. *"As for their rings, they were so high that they were dreadful; and their rings were full of eyes round about them four"* (verse 18).

Imagine a wheel within a wheel—and that the wheels are actually eyes. These four-faced living creatures had eyes all around them. Again, I believe that is why the apostle Paul found it impossible to describe what he saw in heaven. God has created what we have never seen before—far beyond what we can comprehend with our limited, human mind.

Both spiritual and physical connections lie between the wheels and the cherubim. *"When those [cherubim] went, these [wheels] went; and when those stood, these stood; and when those were lifted up from the earth, the wheels were lifted up over against them: for the spirit of the living creature was in the wheels"* (verse 21).

And *"the likeness of the firmament upon the heads of the living creature was as the color of the terrible crystal stretched forth over their heads above"* (verse 22).

The average person never thinks about angels this way, but picture: *"Under the firmament were their wings straight, the one toward the other: every one had two, which covered on this side, and every one had two, which covered on that side, their bodies"* (verse 23).

A MIGHTY NOISE

As the cherubim moved forward, Ezekiel heard a sound his ears had never before experienced. In his own words he describes the picture unfolding before him: *"When they went, I heard the noise of their wings, like the noise of great waters, as the voice of the Almighty, the voice of speech, as the noise of an host"* (verse 24).

There were so many of these cherubim that the movement of their wings must have sounded like the rushing waters of Niagara Falls, or as a great chorus of voices magnifying the Lord. A mighty noise erupted! But when they stood still and let down their wings, the loud sound ceased. Ezekiel was able to hear a voice coming from over their heads. He saw a throne that looked like a sapphire stone, and *"Upon the likeness of the throne was the likeness as the appearance of a man above upon it"* (Ezekiel 1:26).

How awesome! I believe he saw multiple lines with thousands of cherubim—upper wings connected, lower wings covering their bodies, fiery wheels beneath them, with eyes looking in every direction.

Above this scene was God Almighty! What was the assignment of these heavenly beings? They were carrying the wondrous glory of God!

CHAPTER 4

THE "LIVING CREATURES"

We now look at an entirely different category of angels, with a distinct function in heaven. In the Greek they are called *zoa*, translated "living creatures."

These angels are similar to cherubim, except they only have one head, and their bodies are full of eyes in front and behind, perhaps hundreds of eyes. The *zoa* are also like the seraphim, in that they each have six wings.

Here's how they are described in John's revelation: *"Before the throne there was a sea of glass like unto crystal: and in the midst of the throne, and round about the throne, were four beasts [living creatures] full of eyes before and behind. And the first beast [or the first zoa creature] was like a lion, and the second beast like a calf, and the third beast had a face as a man, and the fourth beast was like a flying eagle"* (Revelation 4:6-7).

The seraphim were seen *above* the throne of God, the cherubim were seen *under* the throne, but the living creatures were *"in the midst...and round about the throne"* (verse 6).

As I mentioned earlier, when Ezekiel described the cherubim, each of them had four faces—that of a man, a lion, an ox, and an eagle. Now, in Revelation we find four separate angelic creatures, each with an individual face. Three of the four faces are the same as those on the cherubim, while the fourth is a calf instead of an ox.

Concerning the wings and eyes of the zoa, *"The four beasts had each of them six wings about him; and they were full of eyes within: and they rest not day and night, saying, Holy, holy, holy, LORD God Almighty, which was, and is, and is to come"* (verse 8).

Like the seraphim as revealed to the prophet Isaiah, they worshiped God, crying, *"Holy, holy, holy"* (Isaiah 6:3). Even today, we use these words as we come into the hallowed presence of the Almighty.

YOUR PRAYERS ARE PRESENTED TO GOD

The events of Revelation 5 are centered around the question asked by an angel with a loud voice: *"Who is worthy to open the book, and to loose the seals thereof?"* (verse 2).

John wrote, *"No man in heaven, nor in earth, neither under the earth, was able to open the book, neither to look thereon. And I wept much, because no man was found worthy to open and to read the book, neither to look thereon"* (verses 3-4).

But one of the 24 elders comforted him, saying, *"Weep not: behold, the Lion of the tribe of Judah, the Root of David, hath prevailed to open the book, and to loose the seven seals thereof"* (verse 5).

It was the Son of God, *"a Lamb as it had been slain"*

(verse 6), who was standing in the midst of the throne, the four living creatures, and the elders. Then Jesus *"came and took the book out of the right hand of him that sat upon the throne"* (verse 7).

Now we see another reference to these four living creatures: *"When he had taken the book [with seven seals], the four beasts [zoa] and four and twenty elders fell down before the Lamb, having every one of them harps, and golden vials full of odours, which are the prayers of saints"* (Revelation 5:8).

The 24 elders mentioned are men, possibly the 12 apostles and the 12 sons of Jacob.

If you look closely you'll discover these angels are not empty-handed. In one hand they carry a harp and in the other a golden vial filled with the prayers of believers. Think of it! Every time you cry out to God, what you say is stored in that container and is presented to the Lord. It is recorded and remembered forever. Hallelujah!

A NEW SONG

Envision what is taking place in heaven! God Almighty is seated on His throne. Above Him are seraphim; below Him are cherubim; and He is surrounded by zoa, living creatures playing their harps for worship and carrying a vial of incense (odors) rising from it to remind God of what His people, the church, have asked for.

As they present your prayers and worship they fall *"before the Lamb"* (verse 8), before Jesus. Not only are the angels prostrate before the Son of God, but also the 24 elders.

After Jesus the Lamb, takes the book from the hand of God, *"they sung a new song, saying, Thou art worthy to take the book, and to open the seals thereof: for thou wast slain, and hast redeemed us to God by thy blood out of every kindred, and tongue, and people, and nation. And hast made us unto our God kings and priests: and we shall reign on the earth"* (Revelation 5:9-10).

The fact that Jesus was slain for the sins of mankind gave Him the authority to break the seals and open the scroll.

You may question, how could the zoa, the angels, be redeemed? They were not men and did not come out of every tribe and tongue.

That is true, but what we find here is the angels identifying with the church by joining the 24 elders in worshiping God and thanking Jesus for shedding His blood on the cross.

That is why, together they could rejoice and sing, " *Worthy is the Lamb that was slain to receive power, and riches, and wisdom, and strength, and honour, and glory, and blessing"* (Revelation 5:12).

SEVEN PLAGUES

Later in John's revelation, when the judgements of God had begun, he saw *"another sign in heaven, great and marvelous, seven angels having the seven last plagues; for in them is filled up the wrath of God"* (Revelation 15:1).

John was shown what looked like a sea made of glass with flames of fire. The victors were standing there, carrying harps and rejoicing that they had triumphed over the Beast (the antichrist) and the number of his name (verse 2).

The angels sang the song of the Lamb, saying, *"Great and marvellous are thy works, Lord God Almighty; just and true are thy ways, thou King of saints"* (verse 3).

Then John watched as the doors of the temple opened

wide and the seven angels carrying the seven plagues appeared. They were dressed in clean, white linen and wore gold vests (verses 5-6).

What happens next is remarkable: *"One of the four beasts (zoa) gave unto the seven angels seven golden vials full of the wrath of God"* (Revelation 15:7).

Remember, in verse 1, John saw *"seven angels having the seven last plagues"* that represented the anger of the Almighty. But now, one of these living creatures approached the seven angels, handing them the seven wrath-filled vials. This tells us that these angels were the angels of judgment. Now remember what was written of the seraphim. After the living creatures gave the vials of judgment filled with the wrath of God to the seven angels, the temple was filled with smoke from the glory of God and *"no man was able to enter into the temple, till the seven plagues of the seven angels were fulfilled"* (verse 8).

"IT IS DONE!"

As they began pouring the contents from their seven vials (Revelation 16), we see a spectacular scene unfolding:

1. The first angel poured out his vial on the earth, *"and there fell a noisome and grievous sore upon the men which had the mark of the beast, and upon them which worshipped his image"* (Revelation 16:2).
2. The second angel poured out his vial on the sea, *"and it became as the blood of a dead man: and every living soul died in the sea"* (verse 3).
3. The third angel poured out his vial upon the rivers, *"and they became blood"* (verse 4).

4. The fourth angel poured out his vial upon the sun, *"and power was given unto him to scorch men with fire"* (verse 8).

5. The fifth angel poured out his vial upon the seat of the beast [the antichrist], *"and his kingdom was full of darkness; and they gnawed their tongues for pain"* (verse 10).

6. The sixth angel poured out his vial upon the great river Euphrates, *"and the water thereof was dried up"* (verse 12).

7. The seventh angel poured out his vial into the air, *"and there came a great voice out of the temple of heaven, from the throne, saying, It is done"* (verse 17).

If you recall, it was the seven vials that contained the prayers of the saints (Revelation 5:8) that were given to the living creatures to pour out judgment and make way for the day when *"the four and twenty elders and the four beasts [zoa] fell down and worshipped God that sat on the throne, saying, Amen; Alleluia"* (Revelation 19:4).

Today, we can thank God for the marvelous work of those angels.

CHAPTER 5

ARCHANGELS OF AUTHORITY

Archangels are a special class of angels who were given a high position of authority by God. The word itself means "chief rulers." In some passages of Scripture they are referred to as "princes."

We read about an archangel heralding the second coming of Christ: *"The Lord himself shall descend from heaven with a shout, with the voice of the archangel, and with the trump of God: and the dead in Christ shall rise first: then we which are alive and remain shall be caught up together with them in the clouds, to meet the Lord in the air: and so shall we ever be with the Lord"* (1 Thessalonians 4:16).

Only three archangels are specifically mentioned by name in Scripture:

1. **Michael**, whose name in Hebrew means "like unto God."
2. **Gabriel**, meaning "man of God."
3. **Lucifer**, which means "light holder."

It is significant that the names of the two, Michael and

Gabriel, end with the suffix *el*, which is Hebrew for God. But Lucifer has no such divine attribute.

Why didn't the Creator give Lucifer a name that was connected to the Almighty? Because God knew the end from the beginning.

In addition to these three, there is also mention of Apollyon, *"the angel of the bottomless pit"* (Revelation 9:11), who some have called an archangel, but there is virtually nothing additional written about him in Scripture.

UNIQUE ASSIGNMENTS

At one time Lucifer had significant control over the earth and our universe. He was equal with Michael and Gabriel, even though each had a different function:

- Michael's assignment was to protect God's people, the Jews, and to fulfill that which concerns Israel.
- Gabriel was to standd in the presence of God, proclaiming His Word.
- Lucifer was, at one time, responsible for praise and worship.

We read in the Bible that Lucifer was covered with jewels and filled with music. God told him, *"You were the seal of perfection, full of wisdom and perfect in beauty. You were in Eden, the garden of God; every precious stone was your covering: the sardius, topaz, and diamond, beryl, onyx, and jasper, sapphire, turquoise, and emerald with gold. The workmanship of your timbrels and pipes was prepared for you on the day you were created"* (Ezekiel 28:12-13, NKJV). As such, he was a living orchestra, a symphony within himself, filling heaven with praise to God.

Lucifer was so powerful that he *"walked up and down in the midst of stones of fire"* (verse 14). He had the authority to walk in the very presence of the Almighty.

This was no ordinary angel. God called Lucifer *"the anointed cherub who covers; I established you; you were on the holy mountain of God"* (verse 14). He certainly was not one of the cherubim described by Ezekiel because he had the position of an archangel, or "chief" angel. However, God gave him the title of *"the anointed cherub"* because he was connected to worship.

THE FALL

Lucifer was the only angelic being in heaven who held two offices—worship leader and "covering cherub," which means he was elevated above others.

Ultimately, these titles and positions caused Lucifer to be filled with enormous pride. In fact, he wanted to be worshiped just like God, which led him to invade heaven because of his jealousy. He was cast out of heaven to the earth. Lucifer also ruled over one-third of all God's holy angels. He corrupted them and they later rebelled against God Himself. This brought about their destructions and Lucifer's fall.

Isaiah describes the event: *"How art thou fallen from heaven, O Lucifer, son of the morning! how art thou cut down to the ground, which didst weaken the nations! For thou hast said in thine heart, I will ascend into heaven, I will exalt my throne above the stars of God: I will sit also upon the mount of the congregation, in the sides of the north: I will ascend above the heights of the clouds; I will be like the most*

High. Yet thou shalt be brought down to hell, to the sides of the pit" (Isaiah 14:12-15).

It is essential to understand that these occurrences were pre-Adamic, before the creation of man. This could not have happened after the Garden of Eden, because when Adam was created, Satan was already on the earth, meaning he had already been cast out of heaven. He was no longer Lucifer, the holy archangel.

God told him that from the day of his creation he was perfect in every way until evil was detected in him. Because of his actions, he turned violent and rebelled against God. God cast this anointed angel out of heaven because his heart was lifted up because of his beauty. He corrupted wisdom to attain worldly fame, and God threw him to the ground (Ezekiel 28:15-17).

The Lord Jesus referred to this when He told His disciples, *"I beheld Satan as lightning fall from heaven"* (Luke 10:18).

Because of his rebellion, Lucifer was permanently banished from heaven.

"REPLENISH" THE EARTH

When God created the earth and mankind, it was the serpent Satan, the fallen Lucifer—who approached Eve to deceive her. Prior to that time the earth was inhabited by beings we today call "demons." I know this may come as a surprise to you, but I believe there was a race on earth before Adam ever lived on it. That is why God said to the first man, *"Replenish the earth, and subdue it"* (Genesis 1:28). Note, the word is not *plenish* but *replenish*. He was saying, "The earth was full, but it is now empty. So fill it up again."

God gave the same directive to Noah after He destroyed the earth with a great flood. When the waters subsided, He told Noah and his sons, *"Be fruitful, and multiply, and replenish the earth"* (Genesis 9:1).

The Almighty also instructed Adam to *"subdue"* the earth (verse 28), which brings us to the question: what was there to subdue if there was no enemy? The Creator said this because Satan and his demons were already present on this planet.

The only conclusion I can come to is that prior to Adam there was an earth filled with inhabitants who were not men, who were not created after the image and likeness of God. The earth was filled with demons and had a fallen archangel ruling over it.

THE THREE HEAVENS

Many Bible scholars point to a gap between the first and second verses of Genesis. Verse one reads, *"In the beginning God created the heaven and the earth."* The Hebrew word for "God" here is *Elohim* (plural),meaning God the Father, God the Son, and God the Holy Spirit." And "beginning" in Hebrew is *barasheet*, which means "in the dateless past."

In addition, the King James Version uses the translation "heaven" as singular, but the Hebrew word is *shamayim* which is plural. The Bible refers to three heavens:

1. The first heaven is our atmosphere, what we can see: *"God called the firmament Heaven"* (Genesis 1:8). This is also described by the psalmist: *"When I consider thy heavens, the work of thy fingers, the moon and the stars, which thou hast ordained"* (Psalm 8:3).

2. The second heaven is where spiritual forces of wickedness reside: *"We wrestle not against flesh and blood, but against principalities, against powers, against the rulers of the darkness of this world, against spiritual wickedness in high places"* (Ephesians 6:12). This is where Satan is now ruling.

3. The third heaven is where God abides. It was described by the apostle Paul, who was *"caught up to the third heaven"* (2 Corinthians 12:2).

THE EARTH BECAME

The second verse of Genesis 1 is eye-opening: *"The earth was without form, and void; and darkness was upon the face of the deep."* Suddenly, we go from perfection—a heaven and earth created by God—to an unsightly, messed up earth.

I thank God for allowing me to be born in Israel where I learned to write and speak Hebrew. It has given me a valuable insight into Scripture that I treasure every day.

There continues to be a theological debate over the meaning of "was" in Genesis 1:2: "The earth was..." In Hebrew, "was" (*hayah*) has two meanings. It can be either "became" or "was" (to already exist). You choose.

If the meaning is "became," there is a gap between verses one and two. If the meaning is "was," there is no gap—no pre-Adamic world. To put it another way, if the verse reads, "The earth *became* without form, and void," then something caused it.

In my study of the scriptures, I side with those who use

"became." Otherwise, the earth God created in Genesis 1 was really a piece of mud He took a lengthy time to develop, and that would be evolutionary. However, if in verse 2 the earth "became" a void, it changes the entire picture. Why? Because the Bible declares, *"God himself...formed the earth and made it; he hath established it, he created it not in vain"* (Isaiah 45:18). Our heavenly Father doesn't create chaos; His work is perfect!

But perfection was destroyed by the fall of Lucifer. That is documented in the book of Job where we are told that God in anger judged the earth: *"He removes the mountains, and they do not know when He overturns them in His anger; He shakes the earth out of its place, and its pillars tremble; He commands the sun, and it does not rise; He seals off the stars"* (Job 9:5-7, NKJV).

Isaiah wrote, *"Behold, the LORD maketh the earth empty, and maketh it waste, and turneth it upside down, and scattereth abroad the inhabitants thereof"* (Isaiah 24:1).

When did God seal up the stars in anger? Not since the days of Adam. When has the earth been turned upside down? Not since the creation of man. These events had to take place *before.*

FACT, NOT FANTASY

After the fall of Lucifer, which caused the perfect world God created to be in disarray, *"without form and void,"* we find something wonderful happening: *"The Spirit of God moved upon the face of the waters"* (Genesis 1:2).

Waters? Where did they come from if there was no

perfect earth? One conclusion is that the water was frozen until God said, *"Let there be light"* (Genesis 1:3). So God was moving on the face of an icy planet, which explains the Ice Age, as evidenced by scholars. How else can you explain the dinosaurs that roamed the earth? Only fossils are left, but you cannot deny their existence.

Scientists, after carbon-dating rocks, conclude the world is billions of years old. Well, if the "became" translation of Genesis 1:2 is correct, there is no argument. It also confirms what Job spoke about when he said God *"commandeth the sun, and it riseth not"* (Job 9:7). The Almighty instantly judged the earth and froze the heavens.

To me, today's science is proving the Bible to be truth. The pre-Adamic world is not mere fantasy; it is fact.

A LEGION OF DEMONS

This brings us to the subject of demons. Are they angels? Impossible. Angelic creatures are not interested in your body; they have their own! Jesus never once said, "You angel, come out!"

When a violent, demon-possessed man who was living among the tombs in Gadarenes approached the Son of God, Jesus commanded, *"Come out of the man, thou unclean spirit"* (Mark 5:8). And he was instantly delivered.

Demons are disembodied spirits that can enter into a body—human or otherwise. In the story mentioned above, the man was tormented by literally thousands of demons. We know this because Scripture records that a demon inside the man spoke to the Lord and asked that he not be tortured.

Jesus demanded, "What is your name?

The demon replied, *"My name is Legion: for we are*

many" (Mark 5:9). A legion is 6,000—an incredible number to reside in one body.

Next, the demons pleaded for the Lord not to banish them from where they operated. Nearby was a large herd of pigs feeding and the devils said, *"Send us into the swine, that we may enter into them"* (verse 12).

That is exactly what Jesus did! But the outcome was worse for the pigs than for the man. They went berserk and the entire herd of 2,000 swine stampeded over a cliff into the sea and drowned (verse 13).

THE GREAT DECEIVER

You may ask, who are these demons? And where did they come from?

We need to remember that Lucifer actually invaded heaven to execute his plan to take God's place: *"Thou hast said in thine heart, I will ascend into heaven, I will exalt my throne above the stars of God: I will sit also upon the mount of the congregation, in the sides of the north: I will ascend above the heights of the clouds; I will be like the most High"* (Isaiah 14:13-14).

Who helped him with this betrayal? Angels and demons who inhabited the earth! Lucifer was the commander of one-third of all the angels in heaven, the ones who rebelled against God.

Satan is referred to in Scripture as a star which fell from heaven to earth (Revelation 9:1). And we are told that *"a third of the stars of heaven"* came with him (Revelation 12:4). *"So the great dragon was cast out, that serpent of old, called the Devil and Satan, who deceives the whole world; he was cast to the earth, and his angels were cast out with him"* (verse 9).

If the devil can convince one-third of all angels to turn against God, be warned. Watch out! Don't let him near you. He is the most manipulating, conniving being in the universe.

Let's recap what we know: (1) Lucifer invaded heaven; (2) God threw him out; (3) he and his angels fell to the earth; and (4) the result was the earth's destruction.

The race of beings that lived in the earth were lost. Their bodies became demons and are still in the world today. The Bible in Jeremiah 4:23-28 describes the identical picture we see in Genesis 1:2, except we are told that animals and cities existed before the destruction took place. And so we conclude that these cities were inhabited with a race we know today as demons and animals that existed in the prehistoric world. God promised destruction in Jeremiah 4:27 that took place in Genesis 1.

CREATION VS. RESTORATION

Creation is described in Genesis 1:1, but what we find beginning with verse 2 is the Creator *restoring* the earth. And for the next several verses we see a word of permission used again and again: *Let. "Let there be light"* (verse 3); *"Let there be a firmament"* (verse 6); *"Let the waters bring forth abundantly"* (verse 20); and so on.

We find restoration continuing until the creation of animals, *"And God created great whales, and every living creature that moveth"* (Genesis 1:21). This was also true regarding man and woman: *"So God created man in his own image, in the image of God created he him; male and female created he them"* (verse 27). Before this, God was restoring the earth to a place of habitation so that animals and

46

humanity could exist.

The reason Satan deceived the first woman was to take back the position of authority he lost when Adam was created. And after the fall of man Satan re-invaded the second heaven (Ephesians 6:12) and still operates from the "heavenlies." And it is from there that he will be cast down to the earth a second time (Revelation 12:9-10). Later, we will discover the role the archangel Michael plays in these astounding events.

In the book of Jude we find Satan arguing with Michael over where Moses' body was buried. *"Yet Michael the archangel, when contending with the devil he disputed about the body of Moses, durst not bring against him a railing accusation, but said, The Lord rebuke thee"* (Jude 9). Remember, the devil was Lucifer prior to the fall.

Why would the devil want to know that burial place? Regarding Moses' grave, we are told that he was buried *"in a valley in the land of Moab...but no man knoweth of his sepulchre unto this day"* (Deuteronomy 34:6).

Satan wanted that information so he could build a shrine at the spot and make it into an idol. The devil's purpose is always to corrupt the things of God.

Please understand, Michael had at least some respect for Lucifer, being that the devil still had a position in the heavenlies, even though a wicked one. In this case, Michael didn't get into a shouting match with Satan. Instead he said, "The Lord rebuke you!"

OUR POWER OVER SATAN

We cannot dismiss the fact that Satan still holds certain

authority as *"prince of the power of the air"* (Ephesians 2:2). When Adam ate of the forbidden fruit in the Garden of Eden, he handed the authority God had given him over to Satan, who has kept it ever since.

Even the Son of God recognized this. In the wilderness, the devil took Jesus up on a high mountain *"and showed Him all the kingdoms of the world and their glory. And he said to Him, "All these things I will give You if You will fall down and worship me"* (Matthew 4:8, NKJV).

Jesus didn't argue with Satan over *"the kingdoms of the world"* but said, *"Away with you, Satan! For it is written, 'You shall worship the LORD your God, and Him only you shall serve'"* (verse 10, NKJV).

Satan's defeat was complete on the cross, but his authority will not be removed until that glorious day when Jesus will return and claim what was accomplished at Calvary. That is when Satan will be thrown into the bottomless pit (Revelation 20:1).

As born again believers, we have power over Satan only in the name of Jesus. As we come in His name—meaning in His office or His stead—we have the authority to command him and paralyze his power. But no angel has such authority because they are not redeemed. For God's power belongs only to His church: *"Behold, I give unto you power to tread on serpents and scorpions, and over all the power of the enemy: and nothing shall by any means hurt you. Notwithstanding in this rejoice not, that the spirits are subject unto you; but rather rejoice, because your names are written in heaven"* (Luke 10:19-20).

UNDERSTANDING THE VISION

I love to read the book of Daniel that tells the story of a

young Jewish boy taken captive into Babylon to serve the king. He fiercely defended his faith and became one of God's prophets.

Daniel had a vision of what was about to happen in the future. What he saw was so powerful that he exclaimed, *"There remained no strength in me"* (Daniel 10:10).

In a deep sleep, with his head on the ground, an angel touched him and said, *"O Daniel, a man greatly beloved, understand the words that I speak unto thee, and stand upright: for unto thee am I now sent. And when he had spoken this word unto me, I stood trembling"* (verse 11).

We know this was the archangel Gabriel because in a previous vision, he said, *"I heard a man's voice...which called, and said, Gabriel, make this man to understand the vision"* (Daniel 8:26).

At another time, while Daniel was fervently crying out to God for the deliverance of the Jewish people, *saying, "The man Gabriel, whom I had seen in the vision at the beginning, being caused to fly swiftly, reached me about the time of the evening offering"* (Daniel 9:21, NKJV).

Daniel calls him "the man" Gabriel. This is significant because it tells us that archangels have no wings. Seraphs, cherubs, and living creatures do have wings, but what Daniel witnessed looked like a man. The "common angels" we will discuss later also possess no wings and have the appearance of men.

We also learn that archangels can travel at amazing speeds because Gabriel had the ability to *"fly swiftly"* (verse 21).

According to Daniel, Gabriel *"informed me, and talked with me, and said, 'O Daniel, I have now come forth to give you skill to understand. At the beginning of your supplications the command went out, and I have come to tell you, for you are greatly beloved; therefore consider the matter, and understand the vision"* (verses 22-23, NKJV).

Archangels have the ability to give us wisdom, understanding, and insight.

UNITED IN FIGHTING EVIL FORCES

In Daniel 10 we find Gabriel arriving to once again help Daniel interpret a vision but explaining that he was delayed because he had been in a battle with the prince of Persia (a satanic prince) for three weeks until Michael came to his assistance (Daniel 10:13). So we learn that archangels unite when fighting evil forces. They are in continual warfare in the fulfillment of God's promises.

Let me point your attention to the fact that Gabriel and Michael, because of their positions, have divine knowledge. As Gabriel told Daniel, *"I will shew thee that which is noted in the scripture of truth: and there is none that holdeth with me in these things, but Michael your prince"* (Daniel 10:21).

Gabriel interpreted Daniel's vision concerning the coming days. It included this prophecy dealing with the Jews and Israel: *"At that time Michael shall stand up, the great prince who stands watch over the sons of your people; and there shall be a time of trouble, such as never was since there was a nation, even to that time. And at that time your people shall be delivered, every one who is found written in the book"* (Daniel 12:1).

THE ARCHANGEL OF ANNOUNCEMENT

In the New Testament it was Gabriel who came to Zacharias and foretold that he and his wife, Elizabeth, would have a son named John (Luke 1:13, 19). It was also Gabriel who was sent by God to Nazareth to tell Mary, *"Hail, thou that art highly favoured, the Lord is with thee: blessed art thou among women...and the angel said unto her, Fear not, Mary: for thou hast found favour with God. And, behold, thou shalt conceive in thy womb, and bring forth a son, and shalt call his name JESUS"* (Luke 1:28,30-31).

Gabriel is an archangel of announcement.

Earlier, I shared the passage of Scripture describing how the Lord will descend from heaven with a shout, *"with the voice of the archangel."* The reason Bible scholars believe this to be Gabriel is because we see him involved in heralding prophetic events (as recorded in Daniel).

VICTORY AHEAD!

During the coming war in the heavens, the archangel Michael plays a pivotal role. As recorded in John's revelation, *"Michael and his angels fought against the dragon [Satan]; and the dragon fought and his angels, and prevailed not; neither was their place found any more in heaven"* (Revelation 12:7-8). That is when Satan and his angels are cast to the earth.

Get ready! There is going to be a war one day between God's angels and Satan's angels, and Michael will lead the angelic hosts of the Almighty to victory!

Please understand that archangels possess power over other angels. In the verse above, Michael and his angels wage war, meaning they belong to his rank and domain. They assist him in fighting for control over the systems of the earth.

Today *"the earth is the LORD'S, and the fulness thereof"* (Psalm 24:1). The "system," however, still belongs to Satan

51

since he continues to rule in the heavenlies (or the second heaven). But praise God, the control of both the earth and its system will be given back to God and His Son will reign forever.

Everything Michael and Gabriel are involved in will bring about the fulfillment of God's plan for the earth.

CHAPTER 6

COMMON ANGELS

Most people talk only of angels that have a direct connection with man. So for the purpose of distinguishing them from the four divisions we have discussed, I call them "common" angels. In truth, however, they are anything but common in nature.

These heavenly beings are given several names in Scripture. For example, Daniel wrote, *"I saw in the visions of my head upon my bed, and, behold, a watcher and an holy one came down from heaven"* (Daniel 4:13). The reason angels are called "watchers" is because their primary job is protection. They are a vital part of God's army guarding His children.

They are also called *"the congregation of the mighty"* (Psalm 82:1).

One of the most powerful titles given to angels is when they are referred to as "sons of the mighty." The psalmist wrote, *"Who in the heaven can be compared unto the LORD? who among the sons of the mighty can be likened unto the LORD?"* (Psalm 89:6).

They are His sons, for He is the Mighty One. This is the same terminology used when the Creator asked Job, *"Where wast thou when I laid the foundations of the earth?....When the morning stars sang together, and all the sons of God shouted for joy?"* (Job 38:4,7).

We know these were angels because they are sons of *Elohim* in this scripture, not sons of *Jehovah*, and there is a distinct difference. When you see "sons" in connection with *Elohim,* it refers to angelic beings, not men.

God has twelve names in the Scriptures, and the first, *Elohim,* or "God the Creator, the Mighty One," is used in Genesis 1. However, when God formed man, we find the term "Lord God," or *Jehovah Elohim* (Genesis 2:7). The difference is that the creation of man involved fellowship, which required a covenant.

Other names for angels include God's "hosts," referring to the army of the Lord. The psalmist wrote, *"Bless ye the LORD, all ye his hosts; ye ministers of his, that do his pleasure"* (Psalm 103:21).

They are also called "elect" angels. Paul, writing to young Timothy, gave this advice: *"I charge thee before God, and the Lord Jesus Christ, and the elect angels, that thou observe these things without preferring one before another, doing nothing by partiality"* (1 Timothy 5:21).

The reason they are "elect" is because the fallen angels (the one-third who fell with Lucifer) were rejected.

We are discussing angels that are so many in number we can't possibly count them all. While we can possibly number seraphim, cherubim, living creatures, and archangels, common angels are innumerable.

THE TRUTH ABOUT ANGELS

Common angels are mentioned in Scripture more than those of any other division, and the Bible details some amazing facts about them.

1. Angels are very intelligent.

A woman, who was trying to persuade King David to reconcile with his son Absalom told him, *"My lord is wise, according to the wisdom of an angel of God, to know all things that are in the earth"* (2 Samuel 14:20).

Absalom killed his brother Amnon as punishment for raping Tamar, another member of the family. And then Absalom became a hunted man and was in exile for three years with the family of the king of Geshur (his mother's father), a neighboring kingdom.

Joab, a nephew of King David and commander of his army, knew that deep down, David still loved Absalom. So he arranged for a woman to come before the king and pretend she was in mourning over the loss of her son, who had been killed by his brother in a quarrel. It was a made-up parallel to what had transpired between Absalom and Amnon. Then she asked David to protect her from those who thought she was defending the surviving son from a murder charge.

King David agreed, saying, "Don't worry. I'll take care of the matter."

Then the woman made one last request. Directly addressing the Absalom situation, she asked. *"Why then have you schemed such a thing against the people of God? For the king speaks this thing as one who is guilty, in that the king does not bring his banished one home again"* (2 Samuel 14:13, NKJV).

David asked her to answer truthfully. He wanted to know so he asked, "Is Joab involved in this?"

The woman admitted that he was, but only because Joab

wanted to see reconciliation and turn things around. It was then that she told David he was wise *"according to the wisdom of an angel of God"* (verse 20) and knew all things.

Angels are extremely well-informed, more so than men. God gifted angels with incredible wisdom we don't have. Humans need education to reach a certain level of knowledge that angels were given at the moment God created them. We grow into our wisdom, but they are wise from the start. Remember, like Adam they were created as full-grown beings.

Regarding the things of earth, angels know only what God reveals to them. For example, it is recorded that they knew when Jesus was resurrected from the dead because the Almighty sent them on a mission:

> *And, behold, there was a great earthquake: for the angel of the Lord descended from heaven, and came and rolled back the stone from the door, and sat upon it. His countenance was like lightning, and his raiment white as snow: and for fear of him the keepers did shake, and became as dead men. And the angel answered and said unto the women, Fear not ye: for I know that ye seek Jesus, which was crucified. He is not here: for he is risen, as he said. Come, see the place where the Lord lay. And go quickly, and tell his disciples that he is risen from the dead; and, behold, he goeth before you into Galilee; there shall ye see him: lo, I have told you . (Matthew 28:2-7)*

Angels know far more than humans; however, they are not all-knowing, because that distinction belongs to God alone.

2. Angels are patient.

Perhaps you recall the story of Balak, the king of Moab, who was so concerned over the approaching armies of Israel that he sent for a man named Balaam to place a curse on the Jews. But God told Balaam not to respond: *"Thou shalt not curse the people: for they are blessed"* (Numbers 22:12).

Anxious, the king sent word again, and Balaam reluctantly headed for the king's palace on a donkey. But on the way God's anger flared, *"and the Angel of the LORD took His stand in the way as an adversary against him"* (verse 22, NKJV).

When the donkey saw the angel on the road brandishing a sword, it veered off course and into a ditch. Balaam immediately began to beat the donkey to get it back on the road again. But as they rode through a vineyard with a fence on either side, the donkey once more saw the angel and ran into the fence, crushing Balaam's foot.

Patiently, the angel blocked the way for the third time making it impossible for Balaam to pass through. When the donkey saw the angel, it sat down. Balaam lost his temper and once again beat the animal with a stick.

Then, by a miracle, God gave speech to the donkey. The animal said to Balaam, *"What have I done to you, that you have struck me these three times?"* (verse 28 NLJV).

God instructed Balaam to continue on, but to be faithful and speak only what was told him. As a result, Balaam blessed God's people instead of cursing them.

It took a calm angel to fulfill the Lord's purpose.

3. Angels are meek.

There have been many books written by individuals who

claim they have had a personal encounter with an angel. One even said an angel drank coffee with him and was playful. Forgive me, but that's not biblical. Angels do not socialize with men.

Yes, they do know how to rejoice. Jesus said, "*There is joy in the presence of the angels of God over one sinner that repenteth*" (Luke 15:10). It's amazing but true that angels even delight over things they don't fully understand.

We also know that they are meek and gentle, holding back their strength. We discover that *"angels, which are greater in power and might, bring not railing accusation against them before the Lord"* (2 Peter 2:11). They are careful with their words.

4. Angels cannot die.

Speaking of those who will be resurrected, Jesus declared, *"Neither can they die any more: for they are equal unto the angels; and are the children of God, being the children of the resurrection"* (Luke 20:36). In other words, those who die in Christ are like the angels—immortal.

As you study the Word you will discover that not one angel has been hurt in a battle or failed to accomplish his mission. They are not only ageless, but eternal.

5. Angels are mighty.

To say that angels are powerful is an understatement. They rolled away heavy stones and unlocked prison gates. Paul wrote to the believers at Thessalonica, *"To you who are troubled rest with us, when the Lord Jesus shall be revealed from heaven with his mighty angels"* (2 Thessalonians 1:7).

They are steady, strong, and more forceful than men. To quote the psalmist, *"Bless the LORD, ye his angels, that excel in strength, that do his commandments, hearkening unto the voice of his word"* (Psalm 103:20).

Their appearance can be awesome. At a time when Israel was under Philistine rule, an angel came to a man named Manoah and his wife. She was barren, but the heavenly being told them she would have a son *"and he shall begin to deliver Israel out of the hand of the Philistines"* (Judges 13:5).

The couple built an altar, lit a fire, and offered a sacrifice to the Lord. The Bible tells us *"that the angel of the LORD ascended in the flame of the altar. And Manoah and his wife looked on it, and fell on their faces to the ground"* (verse 20). That's how overpowering the presence of an angel can be.

As promised, a son was born and his name was Samson.

6. Angels are obedient.

Please read the last portion of Psalm 103:20 again. Not only do God's angels "excel in strength," but they obey His commands, responding to His orders.

To "excel" means that strength is multiplied through prayer. And in the next verse we find these words: *"Bless ye the LORD, all ye his hosts; ye ministers of his, that do his pleasure"* (verse 21).

As we discovered previously, angels hear His Word from you: *"To the intent that now unto the principalities and powers in heavenly places might be known by the church the manifold wisdom of God"* (Ephesians 3:10). You limit the power of angels when you speak negative, complaining, unbelieving words instead of speaking what God has declared.

Please receive this into your spirit. The reason we see so few angels today is because God's people fail to release them through the spoken Word. It is so simple. When you voice the Word of God, you allow angels to enter into the spiritual battle. And the ability to open the doors for angels is yours for the asking. The apostle Paul said, *"The word is nigh thee, even in thy mouth, and in thy heart: that is, the word of faith, which we preach"* (Romans 10:8).

So when you pray and confess the Word you are releasing angels. Wow! How powerful!

Let's look again at what happened when war broke out in the heavenlies. The Bible tells us that *"They overcame him by the blood of the Lamb, and by the word of their testimony"* (Revelation 12:11). Who are *they*? We read about the hostilities, but who is involved in the conflict besides the angels? You are!

In this great battle, Satan and his angels are defeated and cast out (verse 9). Then we learn, *"I heard a loud voice saying in heaven, Now is come salvation, and strength, and the kingdom of our God, and the power of his Christ: for the accuser of our brethren is cast down, which accused them before our God day and night"* (verses 10).

It is true that Michael and his angels were fighting the war, but the church is also involved—by the blood of the Lamb and by *"the word of their testimony"* (verse 11).

It could not be the angels applying the blood, because they don't know how. They have not been washed by the precious blood. Then we read, *"They loved not their lives unto the death"* (verse 11). Well, since it is established that angels cannot die, and the saints were involved in prayer, you and I are engaged in this final conflict.

We must depend on His Word, pray the promises of God,

and then watch what happens. The Word spoken through your lips releases angels.

7. Angels are limited in knowledge.

When the angelic beings were created before the formation of the earth, they were given the wisdom and knowledge they needed to function on behalf of God. Yet, in some areas, they have limited knowledge. For example, they don't know when Christ will return to earth. Jesus told His disciples, *"Of that day and that hour knoweth no man, no, not the angels which are in heaven, neither the Son, but the Father"* (Mark 13:32).

We need to also remember that Peter spoke about their desire to increase their understanding of the mysteries of redemption *"now reported unto you by them that have preached the gospel unto you with the Holy Ghost sent down from heaven; which things the angels desire to look into"* (1 Peter 1:12).

They have a hunger to know more and learn by watching believers. The apostle Paul wrote that *"the manifold wisdom of God might be made known by the church to the principalities and powers in the heavenly places, according to the eternal purpose which He accomplished in Christ Jesus our Lord"* (Ephesians 3:10-11, NKJV).

Because of that, think of your responsibility to angelic beings. The day will come when you will judge angels. Paul asked, *"Know ye not that we shall judge angels?"* (1 Corinthians 6:3). God never gave them authority over you; He gave you authority over them.

These angels cannot say with tears in their eyes, "Jesus, I love You." There's no mention of angels weeping. And we do not read of an angel in the presence of God being filled with the Holy Spirit. That is because there is no relationship—the Spirit was given to "those who believe." And since they have never sinned, they can't understand redemption. There was not even a plan to redeem the angels who fell with Lucifer.

Because they were not created in the likeness and image of God, it is impossible for angels to know Him as we do. After all, you cannot have fellowship with a creature that is not of your likeness or your nature. However, because you and I were created in God's image, we have the privilege to know the Creator intimately.

8. Angels can appear visibly and invisibly.

After the Resurrection, Mary looked in the sepulcher *"and she saw two angels in white sitting, one at the head and the other at the feet, where the body of Jesus had lain"* (John 20:12, NKJV). They were visible to her.

At other times, angels are in our midst and are not even recognized. The Bible counsels, *"Be not forgetful to entertain strangers: for thereby some have entertained angels unawares"* (Hebrews 13:2). It is possible that you may be in the presence of an angel and not know it. So don't blindly ignore those you are unfamiliar with.

In the case of Balaam and the donkey, mentioned earlier, the angel was invisible to Balaam but visible to the animal (Numbers 22).

9. Angels can travel at incredible speeds.

Angelic beings can move much faster than our minds can comprehend. As the prophet Ezekiel saw in his vision, *"The living creatures ran and returned as the appearance of a flash of lightning"* (Ezekiel 1:14). Now that is fast!

Jacob, on his journey to Haran, was camping out one night with a stone for a pillow. As he drifted into sleep, He had an amazing dream: *"A stairway was set on the ground and it reached all the way to the sky; angels of God were going up and going down on it"* (Genesis 28:12).

Angels can travel from earth to heaven in the blink of an eye. John wrote, *"I beheld, and heard an angel flying through the midst of heaven"* (Revelation 8:13).

When Jesus chose Nathanael (also known as Bartholomew) to be one of His disciples, the man was shocked that the Lord knew so much about him. Jesus told this chosen one, *"You will see greater things than these...Most assuredly, I say to you, hereafter you shall see heaven open, and the angels of God ascending and descending upon the Son of Man"* (John 1:51, NKJV).

Since angels are not limited to time and space they can fulfill their assignment with astonishing speed.

10. Angels have their own language.

According to the apostle Paul, angels speak in a language that is different from man's. As he told the believers at Corinth, *"Though I speak with the tongues of men and of angels, and have not charity, I am become as sounding brass, or a tinkling cymbal"* (1 Corinthians 13:1).

We are not told what language angels communicate in, but I can guarantee you it is a heavenly one!

CHAPTER 7

THE AWESOME WORK OF ANGELS

According to a 2008 study by the Pew Forum, 68 percent of Americans believe in angels (*Christianity Today*, 6/23/2008). But if you begin asking people, "Exactly what do angels do?" you would receive a wide variety of answers.

When you delve into God's Word, however, you discover that angels have two major responsibilities: (1) they minister before God and (2) they minister to those who have been born again.

Regarding their service to God Almighty, the prophet Daniel had a vision of God sitting on His throne and *"a thousand thousands ministered to Him; ten thousand times ten thousand stood before Him"* (Daniel 7:10, NKJV). As the psalmist wrote, *"Bless the LORD, ye his angels....ye ministers of his, that do his pleasure"* (Psalm 103:20-21).

The second of their duties is directed to the believers: *"Are they [angels] not all ministering spirits, sent forth to minister for them who shall be heirs of salvation?"* (Hebrews 1:14). All means *all* which includes seraphs, cherubs, zoas, archangels, and common angels.

Keep in mind that angels do not belong to the world and are not sent to assist the unbeliever. For this reason, when I hear quasi-religious New Age adherents talk about "my angel," I take exception. In many cases, what they are referring to as angels are actually demons.

Since angels are "spirits" and not humans, they cannot fully identify with you and me. They can't relate to what we are going through. Also, as spirits they have no souls and cannot understand the concept of love—either for you or for God. That is why angels have a curiosity concerning the things of salvation. They are unable to grasp the reason God sent His Son to earth to die for humanity.

Angels neither love nor hate. They're simply spirits appointed by God to minister not *to* but *for* the heirs of salvation. They cannot impart anything *to* you, such as laying on hands for men or women to receive the Holy Spirit or to be healed. But they can deliver a message from the Lord that will bless you; and they can tell you what God is about to do on your behalf.

Angels do not do your bidding but are dispatched by God to minister to believers.

THE ASSIGNMENTS OF ANGELS

It's thrilling to think what these heavenly ambassadors do for God's children. Let's look at their specific missions.

1. Angels give believers protection.

If you are in danger they are sent to your aid. Remember, this protection is not for the sinners but for the saints. While it is true that God's mercy extends beyond anything we can believe, according to the Word, angels are dispatched only to the sons and daughters of God who have been adopted through salvation.

Talk about protection coverage! We have heavenly bodyguards—security on all sides. *"The angel of the LORD encampeth round about them that fear him, and delivereth them"* (Psalm 34:7). Even better, God has directed these celestial beings to provide total safety: *"He shall give his angels charge over thee, to keep thee in all thy ways"* (Psalm 91:11).

When Herod was persecuting followers of Christ, he threw Peter into prison, planning to display and humiliate him in a public trial after Passover. But one night while the apostle was sleeping, bound with chains between two guards *"an angel of the Lord stood by him, and a light shone in the prison; and he struck Peter on the side and raised him up, saying, 'Arise quickly!' And his chains fell off his hands"* (Acts 12:7, NKJV).

The angel told Peter to put on his shoes, grab his coat, and follow him to freedom. Even though Peter thought he was having a vision, he fled with the angel (verse 9). They made it to the iron gate that led to the city, which opened of its own accord. Peter was safe on the streets before the angel left him.

Scripture records, *"When Peter had come to himself, he said, 'Now I know for certain that the Lord has sent His angel, and has delivered me from the hand of Herod and from all the expectation of the Jewish people'"* (verse 11, NKJV).

Often, when one of God's angels comes to your rescue, you won't realize it at the time. The truth of the situation will

67

dawn on you later. You may be driving on the highway and suddenly your car swerves to avoid a terrible accident. It all happens so quickly you don't know what is going on. But a few minutes later you exclaim, "Ahh...God just saved my life!"

Think back on the times the Lord has sent guardian angels for your protection.

I can still recall the moment I heard the pilot say, "We're in trouble!"

Those scary words woke me from my sleep. We were in a small single engine Cessna at 11,000 feet, returning to Orlando from Naples, Florida, in May 1983 about 1 a.m. The sky was pitch black and there were six of us on board.

"I think we are out of fuel," the concerned pilot told us as the engine sputtered and stopped. I could feel my heart pounding against my rib-cage and thought, "God in heaven, I could be with You any minute." Then I began to ask myself, "Am I ready? Am I ready?"

When facing death, that question becomes most powerful. I knew that my answer could leave no room for doubt. Was I ready for eternity?

If you find yourself in the same situation what will you be asking? Are you ready?

As the plane was falling and the pilot was anxiously searching for an emergency landing site, suddenly my mind flashed back to an event that happened eight months earlier.

In September 1982, my father, Costandi, passed away. At the funeral home, the director approached me and said, "Reverend Hinn, your father needs a necktie. Could you get one for him?"

Immediately, I took off the tie I was wearing and handed

it to the mortician. Later, after the funeral service, I was standing before the coffin at the cemetery. As they were lowering the casket of my dear father into the ground, an incident happened that I had almost dismissed from memory. But now as the plane was plummeting, I remembered it all too clearly.

As the pallbearers lowered the coffin, I experienced something quite unusual. Even though I had given my necktie to my father, I suddenly felt a tightening around my throat, as if my own necktie was choking me. I then heard a voice say, You will be dead in one year.

I immediately replied out loud, "No, I won't." When Satan speaks, you had better talk back, even if people are around.

I looked upward toward the sky and said, "God in heaven, the devil can't do that!" And instantly I heard the unmistakable voice of the Holy Spirit. The words He spoke were all I needed. The Spirit softly whispered, "I won't let you die."

Now, on the plane, I remembered those words: "You will be dead in one year!" But I also recalled the reassuring voice of the Holy Spirit.

It took just a second for the entire scene to flash through my mind. Then the peace of God washed over me like a warm blanket and I knew I would not die. I blurted out to the other nervous passengers, "Don't worry. We're going to be all right. The Lord just told me!" For I'd heard His voice again on that plane.

Usually, I am excitable, but at that particular moment I became calm. Without the roar of the engine, the silence was deafening in the plane. The pilot spotted an airstrip near

Avon Park, Florida, and did his best to maneuver the troubled craft to the runway. But with no power it became impossible—and he missed his target.

The plane crashed.

We smashed into a tree and the small aircraft rolled over four times. It was totally demolished—the wheels were ripped off and remained in the tree. The fuselage was so damaged that an onlooker would doubt there could be any survivors. The engine was torn from its housing and we hung upside down.

The door of the plane had disappeared as I crawled out to realize that there was not a scratch on my body. Thank God, I was unharmed.

In the darkness, I began to run in circles for help, not knowing where I was or what direction to go. All I knew was that we were in the middle of a farm. Then I thought, "What in the world am I doing?" I had better go back and help the other passengers."

I ran back to the plane to discover that I was the only one who had escaped injury. The heads of the pilots were jutting through the broken windshield. They were making horrible sounds as I tried to pull them out of the wreckage, but the twisted metal was wrapped around them, making it impossible. Another passenger, a businessman, had injuries to his head, and it was apparent that his eye had popped out of the socket. I reached over and pushed his eye back into place in the name of the Lord.

Miraculously, not one person was killed in the crash. As the ambulance was approaching the site—which seemed to take forever—I began to cry, "Oh Lord, the devil wanted to kill me, but Your angel was by my side. You alone have preserved me because You have a purpose for my life. Otherwise, I would be dead right now. Thank You, Lord."

Later I learned that at the exact moment our plane was experiencing engine trouble, a woman was awakened from her sleep in California. She told the story of how God woke her, saying, "Benny Hinn is in danger! Pray!" She added, "The devil wanted to snuff out your life!"

How well I knew it!

I will never forget the tension-filled moment when I asked, "Am I ready?" In my heart of hearts I knew that I was, and I also understood that God was not finished with my assignment on earth. Earlier, the Holy Spirit had given me the assurance, and now an angel of protection was guarding my life.

2. Angels serve God's saints.

I have always been fascinated by the amazing account of what happened to the prophet Elijah after the showdown with the 450 prophets of Baal on Mount Carmel. Each side was to prepare a sacrifice, and Elijah said, *"Call ye on the name of your gods, and I will call on the name of the LORD: and the God that answereth by fire, let him be God"* (1 Kings 18:24). Eager to prove the other side wrong, they mutually agreed to do this.

After the prophets of Baal failed in their attempt to call fire down from heaven, it was Elijah's turn. He placed a sacrifice on the altar, then prayed, *"LORD God of Abraham, Isaac, and of Israel, let it be known this day that thou art God in Israel, and that I am thy servant, and that I have done all these things at thy word. Hear me, O LORD, hear me, that this*

71

people may know that thou art the LORD God, and that thou hast turned their heart back again" (verses 36-37).

Scripture records that the fire of the Lord fell and consumed not only the sacrifice but the wood, the stones, the dust, and the water in the trench around it. When the people saw this *"they fell on their faces: and they said, The LORD, he is the God; the LORD, he is the God"* (verse 29).

In his zeal for God, Elijah had all 450 prophets of Baal killed. That took place during the reign of Ahab, who told his wife, Jezebel, about the massacre. Shortly thereafter, Jezebel warned the prophet that she was going to kill him.

We then find Elijah fleeing, walking a day's journey into the wilderness where he *"sat down under a juniper tree: and he requested for himself that he might die; and said, It is enough; now, O LORD, take away my life; for I am not better than my fathers"* (1 Kings 19:4).

After wallowing in a sea of self-pity and discouragement, Elijah slept under a juniper tree where *"an angel touched him, and said unto him, Arise and eat. And he looked, and, behold, there was a cake baken on the coals, and a cruse of water at his head. And he did eat and drink, and laid him down again"* (verses 5-6).

When the angel returned for the second time, he told Elijah, *"Arise and eat; because the journey is too great for thee"* (verse 8).

Did you know that angels can cook? According to this passage they can at least make angel food cake! It must have been nutritious, because *"he went in the strength of that food forty days and forty nights as far as Horeb, the mountain of God"* (verse 8, NKJV). That's over 300 miles through the Sinai desert!

If you look at a map of Israel, you'll find he began his journey at Mount Carmel (where the fire fell) in the northern part of the nation near today's city of Haifa. Then he walked to Beersheba, down in the Negev desert. After his miraculous meal, he headed for Mount Horeb. That totals at least 450 miles. But he wasn't alone on his journey, because angels were with him every step of the way.

As a child of God, you are never walking by yourself. Angels are commanded by the Lord to serve His saints. If you are called by God for a divine assignment, these heavenly beings will be by your side.

God will send angels to go ahead of you, to prepare the way, just as He did for Abraham's servant, who was on a mission to find a wife for Isaac. In Mesopotamia, he told the family of Rebekah, *"[Abraham] said to me, The LORD, before whom I walk, will send his angel with thee, and prosper thy way; and thou shalt take a wife for my son of my kindred, and of my father's house"* (Genesis 24:40).

She was God's chosen wife for Isaac.

Angels appeared many times during the struggles of Israel during Old Testament days. Once, when they were being oppressed by the Midianites, a young man named Gideon was threshing wheat when an *"angel of the LORD appeared unto him, and said unto him, The LORD is with thee, thou mighty man of valour"* (Judges 6:12).

This statement came as quite a shock to Gideon, who didn't consider himself a warrior. He argued that if God was with him, why were they suffering at the hands of the enemy? So the angel continued, *"Go in this thy might, and thou shalt save Israel from the hand of the Midianites: have not I sent thee?"* (verse 14).

Even though he considered himself least in his father's house, Gideon followed the instructions: *"When Gideon perceived that he was an angel of the LORD, Gideon said, Alas, O Lord GOD! for because I have seen an angel of the LORD face to face. And the LORD said unto him, Peace be unto thee; fear not: thou shalt not die"* (verses 22-23).

This unlikely man led Israel to one of its greatest victories.

Angels encourage men and women of faith, and they are our "fellow servants" (Revelation 22:9).

3. Angels shield us from danger.

Daniel was a Jew exiled to Babylon during the days of King Nebuchadnezzar. But because of his unique ability to interpret dreams, he was elevated to a position of prestige in the kingdom. After both Nebuchadnezzar and his son, Belshazzar, were removed from office by God Himself—in direct fulfillment of Daniel's dream interpretations—Daniel was promoted to governor of the entire country.

As you can imagine, the princes and lower level governors were extremely jealous, so they conspired together to find a way to get rid of Daniel, a man of prayer who worshiped the true and living God. These men flattered the new king, Darius, by having him issue the following unconditional decree: *"Whosoever shall ask a petition of any God or man for thirty days, save of thee, O king, he shall be cast into the den of lions"* (Daniel 6:7).

When Daniel heard the edict had been made official, he was not intimidated and continued to pray as he had always done. The upstairs windows of his house opened toward Jerusalem, and three times each day he knelt in prayer at that spot, praising and worshiping the Almighty.

As a group, these men deliberately spied on Daniel and found him praying to the God of heaven. They rushed back to King Darius and asked, "Didn't you sign a decree forbidding anyone to pray to any god or man except you for the next thirty days? And if a person is caught disobeying, won't they be thrown into the lions's den?"

"Absolutely, he replied. "The decree stands!"

Then the conspirators said, *"Daniel, which is of the children of the captivity of Judah, regardeth not thee, O king, nor the decree that thou hast signed, but maketh his petition three times a day"* (Daniel 6:13).

Their devious scheme was accomplished.

King Darius tried in vain to find a way to spare Daniel from punishment, but the situation was hopeless. There was no other choice but to live up to his word and throw him to the lions. A large stone was placed over the opening of the den and the king sealed it with his signet ring.

That night Darius couldn't sleep. As the sun was coming up he ran to the lion's den and anxiously called out, *"O Daniel, servant of the living God, is thy God, whom thou servest continually, able to deliver thee from the lions?"* (verse 20).

Daniel replied, *"My God hath sent his angel, and hath shut the lions' mouths, that they have not hurt me"* (verse 22).

He was protected by an angel. Praise God!

Immediately, the king ordered that Daniel be removed from the den, and the Bible records that there was not one scratch on him (verse 23).

What happened to his accusers? They were thrown into

the same den and the lions tore them to pieces.

Immediately King Darius issued the new decree that *"in every dominion of my kingdom men must tremble and fear before the God of Daniel. For He is the living God, and steadfast forever; His kingdom is the one which shall not be destroyed, and His dominion shall endure to the end. He delivers and rescues, and He works signs and wonders in heaven and on earth, who has delivered Daniel from the power of the lions"* (Daniel 6:26-27, NKJV).

Praise God! And the same God who protected Daniel will guard and watch over you! When you pray and ask the Lord for help, He dispatches angels to deliver you from the enemy: *"Let them be as chaff before the wind: and let the angel of the LORD chase them"* (Psalm 35:5).

4. Angels strengthen you in trials.

Following Christ's encounter with Satan on the Mount of Temptation, after the devil left *"behold, angels came and ministered unto him"* (Matthew 4:11). They gave Jesus strength for His earthly assignment that was about to begin.

Later, when the Lord was facing the greatest trial of His life, He went to the Garden of Gethsemane and found a place of seclusion to pray alone. There, Jesus looked up to heaven and said, *"Father, if thou be willing, remove this cup from me: nevertheless not my will, but thine, be done. And there appeared an angel unto him from heaven, strengthening him"* (Luke 22:43).

As a result, He prayed even more fervently: *"Sweat, wrung from him like drops of blood, poured off his face"* (verse 44).

On earth, Jesus was the Son of God, yet He was also a Man: *"We have not an high priest which cannot be touched with the feeling of our infirmities; but was in all points tempted like as we are"* (Hebrews 4:15).

Just as angels came to minister to Christ, they are also ready to empower you and me, regardless of what trials we are going through.

5. Angels bring answers to prayer.

The moment you begin to pray, angels are listening. They stand ready to assist God in bringing the answer exactly when it is needed.

In the marvelous story of Daniel, when he was pouring out his heart and interceding for the people of Israel, an angel appeared before him, saying, *"At the beginning of your supplications the command went out, and I have come to tell you, for you are greatly beloved; therefore consider the matter, and understand the vision"* (Daniel 9:22-23, NKJV). In other words, he had no sooner started to pray than the answer was given, delivered by an angel.

Talk about instant communication! The minute you start praying, God gives the "Go" signal in heaven.

Not long after, Daniel was talking to God, asking Him for the interpretation of a vision, when an angel stood before him and said, *"Do not fear, Daniel, for from the first day that you set your heart to understand, and to humble yourself before your God, your words were heard; and I have come because of your words"* (Daniel 10:12, NKJV).

When we fail to call on the Lord we limit His angels, because they respond to prayer. May God Almighty develop in you a mighty hunger for prayer so you will see the supernatural at work in every aspect of your life.

6. Angels impart God's will.

Your heavenly Father doesn't send His angels to entertain you with a harp recital or to sing songs. Their purpose is far greater. In fact, many Christians have never considered that angels help them know God's will for their lives.

Let's look at what happened in Jerusalem after the Day of Pentecost. People were being saved, healed, and delivered, and the church was expanding rapidly. This confounded the religious leaders, and the Sadducees began arresting the apostles and putting them in jail. But *"the angel of the Lord by night opened the prison doors, and brought them forth, and said, Go, stand and speak in the temple to the people all the words of this life"* (Acts 5:19-20).

The angels were giving divine assistance, helping to fulfill the will of God for His people. According to the Great Commission we are to *"go...and teach all nations, baptizing them in the name of the Father, and of the Son, and of the Holy Ghost: teaching them to observe all things whatsoever I have commanded you"* (Matthew 28:19-20).

The world will attempt to stop you from hearing—let alone obeying—God's directive, but rejoice in the fact that angels will assist you in carrying out this divine mission. If you are committed and determined to obey God, all the devils in hell can't stop you. Why? Because the angels of the Lord will make sure you complete what God has ordered.

The exodus of the children of Israel from Egypt is one of the greatest adventures ever recorded, but it all began when

God sent an angel to get the attention of one man: *"Moses kept the flock of Jethro his father in law, the priest of Midian: and he led the flock to the backside of the desert, and came to the mountain of God, even to Horeb. And the angel of the LORD appeared unto him in a flame of fire out of the midst of a bush: and he looked, and, behold, the bush burned with fire, and the bush was not consumed"* (Exodus 3:1-2).

In response to God's call, Moses said, "Here am I."

It was the will of the Almighty for the Israelites to embark on their journey toward the Promised Land *and the angel of God* led the way (Exodus 14:19).

Today, angels are under the authority of Christ as they continue the divine work of seeing the Father's will accomplished. Jesus is *"on the right hand of God; angels and authorities and powers being made subject unto him"* (1 Peter 3:21-22).

7. Angels can execute judgment.

I want to share a story I heard several years ago of a young girl who lived in a Christian camp in Africa. One night, a neighboring tribe of people who practiced witchcraft came to attack them.

The families were frightened and panic stricken, but the girl fell to her knees and began to pray.

The invaders were running wild, ready to kill everyone in the camp, when suddenly they stopped in their tracks and made a hasty retreat. The tables were turned and they ran away in fear.

The Christian families couldn't believe their eyes. What happened? Why did they flee? they wondered.

A few days later, one of the tribal leaders returned to the camp alone, wanting to make peace.

"Why did you run?" they asked him.

"Because of the army you had here protecting you," he replied.

"What army?" the shocked Christians asked.

"The soldiers that surrounded your camp. There were thousands and thousands of men on horses."

"We don't have an army or any horses" the surprised Christians told him. "You must be mistaken. All we saw were your angry tribesmen."

Without a doubt, God caused the eyes of the attackers to see the angels of God surrounding the camp. But no one inside the compound saw any of this. It was the fervent prayers of one small child that turned the situation around.

I believe that if the invaders had continued their raid, they would have been the victims of the judgement of these angels.

Heavenly beings do not act on their own, but on direct orders from God Almighty. Even though most people like to think of them as sweet and warm, dressed in white with fluttering wings, and a tinsel halo, they are on a serious mission. They can execute judgment on behalf of the Lord. Scripture tells us, *"If the word spoken by angels was stedfast, and every transgression and disobedience received a just recompence of reward, how shall we escape, if we neglect so great salvation; which at the first began to be spoken by the Lord, and was confirmed unto us by them that heard him?"* (Hebrews 2:2).

In this passage God is letting us know that if Israel was judged for disobeying the words of an angel (remember, the

Almighty gave the law to Moses through the hand of an angel), how will we escape if we disobey Him? For our salvation did not come through an angel, our salvation came through the Son of God who died for us.

It was the angel of the Lord who was a go-between to lead the children of Israel through the wilderness. Angels were not only sent to deliver God's message to His people, but also to judge. They've even been given the authority to destroy God's enemies, which they did on a number of occasions.

Let me remind you of what took place in the sin-filled cities of Sodom and Gomorrah. Abraham's nephew, Lot, was sitting at the gate of Sodom when two angels appeared. He invited them to spend the night at his home, but the townsmen surrounded Lot's house and started breaking down his door to find out who these strangers were.

The angels *"smote the men that were at the door of the house with blindness"* (Genesis 19:11). Then they told Lot and his family to leave Sodom immediately, saying, *"The LORD hath sent us to destroy it"* (verse 13). But the angels said the destruction would not happen unless Lot left. That is a direct response to Abraham's intercession on Lot's behalf much earlier. When the same angels visited Abraham and turned toward Sodom, the man of faith looked up to God and prayed, *"Wilt thou also destroy the righteous with the wicked?"* (Genesis 18:23).

Lot and his family were spared as fire and brimstone rained down from heaven.

We also find angels at work during the reign of King Hezekiah. The Assyrian army had threatened to invade Jerusalem. When Hezekiah heard of the impending attack, he tore his clothes, covered himself with sackcloth, and went to the house of God to pray. He was one of the most God-fearing kings of Israel.

As the vast armies of Assyria advanced and were preparing to attack, Hezekiah prayed, *"O Now therefore, O LORD our God, I beseech thee, save thou us out of his [the King of Assyria] hand, that all the kingdoms of the earth may know that thou art the LORD God, even thou only"* (2 Kings 19:19).

The prophet Isaiah spoke the words of God when he said, *"I will defend this city, to save it, for mine own sake, and for my servant David's sake"* (verse 34).

What took place next was an absolute miracle: *"It came to pass that night, that the angel of the LORD went out, and smote in the camp of the Assyrians an hundred fourscore and five thousand: and when they arose early in the morning, behold, they were all dead corpses"* (verse 35).

That's an imposing army of 185,000 men slain by one angel! Without question, in answer to prayer, angels execute judgement.

What crisis do you face? What causes you to panic and be full of fear? God is telling you to get on your knees and pray, because there's not an attack of the enemy the Lord can't defeat with just one of His angels.

We've already discussed how Herod threw Peter into prison and that he was freed by an angel. But that's not the end of the story.

When the king's jailers could not explain how Peter had escaped, Herod ordered their execution, then went to his palace in Caesarea. There, he was surrounded by admiring citizens who flattered his ego. After one oration, the people shouted, *"It is the voice of a god, and not of a man"* (Acts 12:22).

God finally had enough of Herod's antagonism and arrogance, so one day while this Christian-hating king was sitting on his throne *"an angel of the Lord struck him, because he did not give glory to God. And he was eaten by worms and died"* (verse 23).

It is dangerous to accept glory for yourself when the rightful owner is God. This evil king was slain by one of God's angels, and justly so.

Again and again in Scripture we see the Lord dispatching heavenly beings against the wicked. Jesus spoke of the end time when *"the Son of man shall send forth his angels, and they shall gather out of his kingdom all things that offend, and them which do iniquity; and shall cast them into a furnace of fire: there shall be wailing and gnashing of teeth"* (Matthew 13:41-42).

Angels are used by the Almighty to fulfill His plans and purposes, even if it involves the judgment of the unrighteous.

8. Angels assist in leading people to Christ.

Perhaps you have poured out your heart to God night after night, praying for a dear friend to be saved, and you felt you were the only one who cared. Think again. In certain instances God will send an angel (or angels) to lead that individual to a place where he or she can find the Lord.

Take the case of Cornelius, captain of the Roman Guard in Caesarea. He was a godly man who was always helping those in need. Then one day, about three o'clock in the afternoon, while this Gentile was praying, he had an amazing vision. He saw *"an angel of God coming in to him, and saying unto him, Cornelius"* (Acts 10:3).

At first he was afraid, but then he gathered the courage to ask, "What do you want?"

The angel explained how his prayers and neighborly acts had brought Cornelius to God's attention. Then he was given these instructions: *"Send men to Joppa, and call for one Simon, whose surname is Peter: He lodgeth with one Simon a tanner, whose house is by the sea side: he shall tell thee what thou oughtest to do"* (verses 5-6).

This entire scene brings back such memories. It is so real to me. As a child, I grew up in Joppa, now called Jaffa, and as kids we used to play down by the docks, just across from the house of Simon the tanner.

When the angel departed, Cornelius told two of his trusted servants and a devoted soldier what had just taken place and sent them off to Joppa, about 30 miles down the coast.

As they were approaching the city, Peter was on Simon's housetop about lunchtime when suddenly he fell into a trance. God showed him what looked like a large blanket being lowered by ropes and it settled to the ground. *"In it were all kinds of four-footed animals of the earth, wild beasts, creeping things, and birds of the air. And a voice came to him, 'Rise, Peter; kill and eat'"* (Acts 10:12-13, NKJV). Peter resisted, saying he had never eaten anything that wasn't kosher, food approved by the Jewish rabbis.

The voice spoke to him a second time: *"What God hath cleansed, that call not thou common"* (verse 13). This happened three times, then the blanket was pulled up to the skies and disappeared.

While Peter was trying to figure out the meaning of all this, the three men sent by Cornelius arrived at the front door asking if a person named Peter was staying there. At the same time, the Spirit whispered to Peter, *"Behold, three men seek thee. Arise therefore, and get thee down, and go with them, doubting nothing: for I have sent them"* (verses 19-20).

Once downstairs, Peter told the men he was the one they were looking for. They explained to him how Cornelius was commanded by an angel to send for him, and that he was to return with them and share whatever he had to say. The next morning the group, including some of Peter's friends from Joppa, journeyed to Caesarea.

The minute Peter entered the house of Cornelius, the military captain fell down and worshiped him. But Peter insisted, *"Stand up; I myself also am a man"* (verse 26).

A large group had gathered and Peter addressed them: *"You know how unlawful it is for a Jewish man to keep company with or go to one of another nation. But God has shown me that I should not call any man common or unclean"* (verse 28, NKJV). But he still wanted to know from Cornelius, "Why did you send for me?"

Cornelius shared the story that while he was praying, an angel came to him, asking that he send for a man named Peter who would visit his home. Then he said, *"Now therefore, we are all present before God, to hear all the things commanded you by God"* (verse 33).

It's important to note that Cornelius didn't know the plan of salvation, or that it was even available for him.

What happened next was a turning point in history. For the first time, the message of Christ was being preached not only to the Jews but to the Gentiles, telling them, *"whosoever believeth in him shall receive remission of sins"* (verse 43).

Cornelius and his household were all saved. And while

Peter was still sharing the Good News, *"the Holy Ghost fell on all them which heard the word"* (verse 44).

Those who accompanied Peter were astonished *"that on the Gentiles also was poured out the gift of the Holy Ghost. For they heard them speak with tongues, and magnify God"* (verses 45-46).

In response to prayer, the angel of the Lord was involved in the salvation of the house of Cornelius. That is why you should never give up or tire of praying for those you love.

9. Angels direct those who minister the Gospel.

The apostle Paul was in a horrible storm on his way to stand trial in Rome. As the ship was battered by the waves and falling apart, he told those on board not to worry: *"There stood by me this night an angel of the God to whom I belong and whom I serve, saying, 'Do not be afraid, Paul; you must be brought before Caesar; and indeed God has granted you all those who sail with you'"* (Acts 28:23-24, NKJV).

An angel also ministered to Philip, the first-century evangelist. During a time of great persecution, after Stephen was stoned and killed for preaching the Gospel, Philip became bold in his testimony and went everywhere proclaiming Christ.

One day *"the angel of the Lord spake unto Philip, saying, Arise, and go toward the south unto the way that goeth down from Jerusalem unto Gaza, which is desert"* (Acts 8:26). Philip did not question why; he just obeyed.

On the way, he met an Ethiopian eunuch who was traveling down the road. The eunuch, in charge of the finances of the queen of Ethiopia, had been on a pilgrimage to Jerusalem and was on his way home. He was riding in a chariot and reading from the words of the prophet Isaiah.

The angel knew that this man needed to hear the Gospel.

The Spirit told Philip to run along-side of the chariot. And when he heard the eunuch speaking Scripture out loud, he asked, "Sir, do you understand what you are reading?"

He answered, *"How can I, except some man should guide me? And he desired Philip that he would come up and sit with him"* (verse 31).

Here is the portion of Scripture the Ethiopian was reading:

He was led as a sheep to the slaughter;
And as a lamb before its shearer is silent,
So He opened not His mouth.
In His humiliation His justice was taken away,
And who will declare His generation?
For His life is taken from the earth. (verses 32-33, NKJV).

The eunuch wanted to know if Isaiah was referring to himself or to some other man. That gave Philip the golden opportunity to share the miraculous story of Christ, who shed His blood for our sins.

Riding in his chariot, the Ethiopian was gloriously saved and wanted to be baptized. Philip responded, " *'If you believe with all your heart, you may.' And he answered and said, 'I believe that Jesus Christ is the Son of God'"* (verse 37, NKJV).

They stopped at a stream and the evangelist baptized the man. When they came out of the water, *"the Spirit of the Lord caught away Philip, that the eunuch saw him no more: and he went on his way rejoicing"* (verse 39). And the

Ethiopian returned to his people with the message of Christ.

That was a fulfillment of a prophetic word given by David when he said, *"Princes shall come out of Egypt; Ethiopia shall soon stretch out her hands unto God"* (Psalm 68:31).

This all came to pass when an angel led a preacher to a man who needed the forgiveness of Christ. Hallelujah!

A similar visitation happened to the apostle Paul. After returning to Jerusalem from one of his missionary journeys, the Jewish religious leaders began to make accusations against him, which led to Paul's arrest. At a public hearing, Paul gave the testimony of his conversion and pleaded that he had done nothing wrong. To wipe his hands of the situation, King Agrippa agreed to send Paul to Rome, where he could make his appeal directly to Caesar.

Still a prisoner, the apostle was placed on a ship headed first to Ephesus. But after being transferred to another vessel in Cyprus, they ran into bad weather and had to dock at the island of Crete.

Paul warned the captain that they should stay where they were, but he wouldn't listen to the advice of a prisoner. As they attempted to make it to another port, gale-force winds and high seas began to severely damage the boat. Paul described the ordeal: *"Because we were exceedingly tempest-tossed, the next day they lightened the ship. On the third day we threw the ship's tackle overboard with our own hands"* (Acts 27:18, NKJV). After several days of riding out this treacherous storm, those on board had given up all hope of making it to shore alive.

Finally, Paul stood before everyone on board and announced, *"Sirs, ye should have hearkened unto me, and not have loosed from Crete, and to have gained this harm and loss. And now I exhort you to be of good cheer: for there shall be no loss of any man's life among you, but of the ship"* (verses 21:22).

How could he know this? He explained, *"For there stood by me this night the angel of God, whose I am, and whom I serve, saying, Fear not, Paul; thou must be brought before Caesar: and, lo, God hath given thee all them that sail with thee"* (verses 23-24).

The angel reassured Paul not to be afraid, because it was God's plan for him to preach the Gospel to Caesar.

On the fourteenth day, what was left of the ship hit a reef and the men swam to shore. From there they traveled to Rome.

You may say, "But that all happened 2,000 years ago. Does the Lord still use angels to direct the steps of those in ministry today?" Of course He does, since *"there is no respecter of persons with God"* (Romans 2:11).

10. Angels appear in dreams.

It's exciting to read the stories of angelic beings in Bible days, but when you personally experience their presence it is life changing!

I can still vividly recall a dream that unfolded while I was sleeping in my bedroom on a cold, chilly night in February 1972. It came out of left field and absolutely stunned me. I was a senior at Georges Vanier Secondary School in Toronto and had not yet given my life to Christ.

In my dream I found myself descending a long, dark stairway. It was so steep I thought I would fall. And it was leading me into a deep, endless chasm.

I was bound by a chain to a prisoner in front of me and a prisoner behind me. I was dressed in the clothing of a convict and there were chains on my ankles and around my wrists. As far as I could see ahead of me and behind me there was a never-ending line of captives.

Then, in the haze of that dimly lit shaft, I saw dozens of small people moving around. They were like imps with strange-shaped ears. I could see their faces, but their forms were barely visible. We were obviously being pulled down the stairway by them, like a herd of cattle to a slaughter-house.

Suddenly, appearing out of nowhere, was an angel of the Lord. It was a wondrous thing to see. The heavenly being hovered just ahead of me, a few steps away. Never in my life had I seen such a sight—a bright and beautiful angel in the midst of a dark, black hole.

As I looked again, the angel motioned with his hand for me to come closer. Then he looked into my eyes and called me out. My eyes were riveted to his, and I began to walk toward him. Instantly, those bonds fell off my hands and feet. I was no longer tied to my fellow prisoners.

Hurriedly the angel led me through an open doorway, and the moment I walked into the light, the celestial being took me by the hand and dropped me on Don Mills Road, right at the corner of Georges Vanier School. He left me just inches from the wall of the school building, right beside a window.

In a second, the angel was gone, and I woke up early and rushed off to school to study in the library before classes began.

As I sat there, not even thinking about the dream, a small

group of students walked over to my table. I recognized them immediately since they had been pestering me with "Jesus talk" for quite some time.

They asked me to join them in their morning prayer meeting in a room just off the library. I thought, well, if I go it will get them off my back.

"All right," I said, and they walked with me into the room. It was a small gathering.

All of a sudden, the entire group lifted their hands and began to pray in some funny foreign language. I didn't even close my eyes. I could hardly blink as the students in their late teens were praising God with unintelligible sounds. I had never heard of speaking in tongues.

What happened next was mind blowing. I was startled by a sudden urge to pray but didn't know what to say. In all of my childhood religious classes I had never been taught the sinner's prayer but I remembered a vision I had of Jesus when I was eleven years old. So I just closed my eyes and uttered the words, "Lord Jesus, come back."

Praise God, He did! I felt a surge of power, cleansing me from the inside out. Jesus became as real to me as life itself. Beyond doubt, I knew something extraordinary happened to me the morning of February 14 in 1972 at 7:50 a.m.

All day long I wiped tears from my eyes. And the only thing I could say was, "Jesus I love You...Jesus I love You."

After the last class, as I walked out the door of the school and down the sidewalk to the corner, I looked at the window of the library and the pieces began to fall into place.

The angel. The dream. It all became so real again.

We must never glibly dismiss the power of a dream, especially when God is involved.

Let's go back to the time of Isaac's son, Jacob. Far from home he describes how *"the angel of God spake unto me in*

91

a dream, saying, Jacob: And I said, Here am I" (Genesis 31:11). Then the angel told him to take his wife and children back to the land of Canaan and reunite with his father, Isaac. What a homecoming it was!

Centuries later, a dream involving an angel took place before the birth of Christ.

Mary and Joseph were engaged to be married when he found out she was pregnant. He knew he could not be the father, since they had not consummated their marriage. But Joseph, not wanting her to be scorned, was looking for a way to hide the upcoming birth.

Then there was a most unusual occurrence. While Joseph was pondering the situation *"the angel of the Lord appeared unto him in a dream, saying, Joseph, thou son of David, fear not to take unto thee Mary thy wife: for that which is conceived in her is of the Holy Ghost"* (Matthew 1:20).

The angel told him the child should be called Jesus, because *"he shall save his people from their sins"* (verse 21). This was a fulfillment of prophecy (verses 22-23).

When Joseph woke from his dream, he *"did as the angel of the Lord commanded him"* (verse 24, NKJV) and married the mother of God's precious Son, Jesus.

Later, for the second time *"the angel of the Lord appeareth to Joseph in a dream, saying, Arise, and take the young child and his mother, and flee into Egypt, and be thou there until I bring thee word: for Herod will seek the young child to destroy him"* (Matthew 2:13).

They fled just in time because Herod commanded the murder of every male child two years old and under who lived in Bethlehem and the surrounding area.

When Herod was dead, there was an angelic visit for the

third time: *"An angel of the Lord appeareth in a dream to Joseph in Egypt, saying, Arise, and take the young child and his mother, and go into the land of Israel: for they are dead which sought the young child's life"* (verses 19-20).

We should never ignore or take lightly dreams involving God's angels. The Lord may be speaking to us, giving direction and sparing our lives.

11. Angels witness our confession.

I believe with all my heart that every time a man, woman, or young person prays for salvation, angels are watching and rejoicing. Even though they don't fully understand redemption, they are celebrating in heaven!

In Jesus' day, the Pharisees and religious scholars criticized the fact that He spent time with people of dubious reputations. They murmured, *"This man receiveth sinners, and eateth with them"* (Luke 15:2).

This led Jesus to ask, "Suppose you had a hundred sheep and one strayed from the fold? Wouldn't you leave the ninety-nine in the pasture and search for the lost one until you rescued it?"

He added, "When you found that lost sheep, I'm sure you would lift it up on your shoulders, and when you arrived home you'd call your friends and neighbors to share the good news." Then Jesus made this profound statement, *"I say unto you, that likewise joy shall be in heaven over one sinner that repenteth, more than over ninety and nine just persons, which need no repentance"* (verse 7).

To drive the point home, He asked them to imagine a woman who has ten coins, but loses one of them. "Won't she light a candle, scour the house, and keep looking until she locates it?" And after finding the coin, she will call her neighbors, asking them to rejoice with her for finding what she had lost. *"Likewise, I say unto you, there is joy in the presence of the angels of God over one sinner that repenteth"* (verse 10).

Angels not only witness the confession of a lost soul, they rejoice in heaven when a person is born again and brought into the fold of the Good Shepherd.

12. Angels are involved in fulfilling prophecy.

God has not forgotten or forsaken His people. In 1948 the Almighty performed one of the mightiest miracles of our age, restoring Israel as a nation. It was almost unbelievable news when the United Nations voted to give the Jews their homeland after there was so much worldwide opposition. Yet, it was a direct fulfillment of prophecy (Amos 9:14-15; Ezekiel 37:10-14).

God said, *"I will bring thy seed from the east, and gather thee from the west; I will say to the north, Give up; and to the south, Keep not back: bring my sons from far, and my daughters from the ends of the earth"* (Isaiah 43:5-6).

I am amazed every time I visit Israel and meet Jews who have returned from Europe and Russia (north), Eastern Arab countries (east) North America (west) and Ethiopia (south). The once-barren desert is blossoming as a rose.

Even the preservation of the Hebrew language is amazing. Think of the millions of immigrants who flooded the shores of America and over time have forgotten their native tongue. Not the Jews! They returned speaking Hebrew, just as prophesied by Jeremiah: *"Thus says the LORD of hosts, the God of Israel: "They shall again use this speech in the land of Judah and in its cities, when I bring back their captivity"* (Jeremiah 31:23).

According to Scripture, the creation of the State of Israel is just a foretaste of a regathering of the Jewish people that will take place after the Tribulation (Matthew 24:21). The day will dawn when angels will have an assignment unlike any the world has known. Jesus spoke about it when He declared that God *"shall send his angels with a great sound of a trumpet, and they shall gather together his elect [Israel] from the four winds, from one end of heaven to the other"* (verse 31).

Many of "God's chosen people" have already migrated to Israel, but one day angelic beings will be released from heaven to find every Jew on earth and bring them back to the Promised Land. Some may have lost contact with their heritage, but the angels have not lost sight of them and know exactly where they are. They will be brought home.

John saw *"the holy city, new Jerusalem, coming down from God out of heaven, prepared as a bride adorned for her husband"* (Revelation 21:2).

In his vision the city sparkled like a precious gem. It had a majestic wall with twelve gates—and an angel standing at each one. On the gates were written the names of the twelve tribes of the sons of Israel. Plus, the wall was set on twelve foundations, and on them were inscribed the names of the twelve apostles of the Lamb (verses 12-14).

At the triumphant second coming of Christ, the heavens will open and angels will accompany the Lord back to earth:

- *"The Son of man shall come in the glory of his Father with his angels"* (Matthew 16:27).
- *"When the Son of man shall come in his glory, and all the holy angels with him, then shall he sit upon the throne of his glory"* (Matthew 25:31).
- *" To you who are troubled rest with us, when the Lord Jesus shall be revealed from heaven with his mighty angels"* (2 Thessalonians 1:7-10).

When the angels descend from on high, they will separate the wheat from the tares—the righteous from the sinners: *"The Son of Man shall send forth his angels, and they shall gather out of his kingdom all things that offend, and them which do iniquity; and shall cast them into a furnace of fire: there shall be wailing and gnashing of teeth. Then shall the righteous shine forth as the sun in the kingdom of their Father"* (Matthew 13:41-43).

I pray you are prepared for these prophetic days ahead.

13. Angels will wage war and defeat Satan.

During the final battle, angels will fight against satanic forces and will be victorious (Revelation 12:7). During this conflict, one angel will have an awesome task: *"I saw an angel come down from heaven, having the key of the bottomless pit and a great chain in his hand. And he laid hold on the dragon, that old serpent, which is the Devil, and Satan, and bound him a thousand years, and cast him into the bottomless pit"* (Revelation 20:1-3).

Satan will be placed in chains so he cannot deceive the nations during the thousand-year reign of Christ on the earth (Revelation 20:4,6).

During the Tribulation an angel will proclaim the Gospel. *"I saw another angel fly in the midst of heaven, having the everlasting gospel to preach unto them that dwell on the earth, and to every nation, and kindred, and tongue, and people, saying with a loud voice, Fear God, and give glory to him; for the hour of his judgment is come: and worship him that made heaven, and earth, and the sea, and the fountains of waters"* (Revelation 14:6-7).

What a crusade that will be!

14. Angels will meet believers and take us to heaven.

Have no fear about your journey to the celestial city. You will not be traveling alone. Angels will be accompanying you and are preparing a great welcome celebration.

Jesus told the story of a wealthy man who spent his days in luxurious living. At his doorstep sat a poor beggar, covered with sores. All he longed for was to eat the scraps from the rich man's table. His best friends were the dogs who came and licked his wounds.

But the God of love saw the impoverished man's pure heart. The Bible says, *"It came to pass, that the beggar died, and was carried by the angels into Abraham's bosom"* (Luke 16:22).

I can see the man being lifted up and carried by angelic beings through the gates of heaven. And as sons and daughters of the King of kings, we can expect the same royal welcome!

PART II

DEMONS

CHAPTER 8

FACE TO FACE WITH DEMONS

It happened in Vancouver, British Columbia, in 1977, just two years after I began preaching the Gospel. I was ministering for Don Gossett in a service held in the ballroom of the Sheraton hotel when a man in front of me suddenly turned into an animal. Yes, an animal!

Never in a million years did I think I would ever see anything like I did that night. The man, the size of a football player, walked out of the audience and stood right in front of me. He transformed from a man into a beast before my eyes. His body was bent over, lines appeared in his face, and he began to growl.

To be honest, it scared the daylights out of me! The man turned completely demonic, not only in his behavior, but physically, in his looks. He was walking and growling like an animal and began to swing his arms around.

At that point in my young ministry, I knew practically nothing about how to cast out devils. I had been content to preach the Gospel and see people saved and healed, but didn't delve into issues regarding the devil or demons.

The only thing I knew instinctively to do was to stretch my hand toward him and pray, "In Jesus' name!" And every time I said this he would back up and then lunge toward me again.

Fear began to rise within me as I watched several grown men attempt to restrain him. But he was throwing them off as if they were small children. When bodies began flying through the air, I ran and hid behind the organ Mrs. Gossett was playing.

He followed me and it took several men to finally pin him down. I left the room disturbed and frightened. I began to pray, "Lord, if You want me to preach again, You'd better tell me what to do about this!"

Immediately, I began to seriously study what the Bible had to say concerning demons and what gives them the authority to do what I had witnessed.

LIKE A SERPENT

Not long after that incident I was preaching for Fred Spring at a Full Gospel Business Men's meeting in Sault Ste. Marie, Ontario. (Fred later became a member of our staff.)

I had been searching God's Word and learning more and more about the function of demons, when suddenly a young man walked to the front of the auditorium and hit the ground. He wasn't a big man like the fellow in Vancouver.

The moment he was on the floor, he began slithering like a snake. At almost the same time bite marks began to appear on the man's arms as if he was being bitten on the inside. Simultaneously, his legs were straight, but his feet were moving rapidly, like the tail of a snake! It was frightening to watch.

Suddenly, the young man stood up, walked over to the big grand piano and lifted it up with one hand as if it were as light as a feather. He then began growling and screaming at everyone present. It shocked me and struck fear into the hearts of the hundreds of people who were watching the scene unfold.

These two events let me know that if I was going to stay in the ministry, I had better learn how to deal with such tormented people.

I started with questions. Where did the devil come from? Why and how did he become the devil? From where did demons originate and how can they possess a body? What is it that causes a person to take on the characteristics of an animal? What gives a person such unnatural strength to pick up a grand piano?

Over the years, we have seen many demonstrations of demonic activity. For example, my staff can tell you that in the country of Jordan we saw a young man's body began to levitate on our crusade platform. As the demons raised him up, we tried to push him back down. This continued for a few moments. Then he began throwing plants and decorations everywhere with a strength that was not natural.

We've certainly seen our share of demonic manifestations. But we have learned there is mighty power in the name of Jesus, a power so great and eternal that no demon can stand before Him. However, many believers do not know how to use the spiritual tools that are available to them to fight the devil. They have not taken the time to find out what the Bible says on the topic. That is why I want to train and equip you to be God's soldiers in this battle. You have authority through the name and blood of Jesus.

It is possible for you to walk into a room and, by your very presence, demons will flee. That is what God's Word declares.

BEYOND BONDAGE

I have been amazed by how little Christians know about demons and demonology. Perhaps it's because so many churches have focused on a seeker-friendly message instead of a well-balanced ministry that includes teaching the depths of God's Word. Rather than preaching about the blood, the cross, heaven, and hell, some pastors would rather tell their congregation how successful they can be by just remaining positive and looking on the bright side of life. It's no different than a motivational talk with a little "God" thrown in.

My friend, first and foremost, it is the unadulterated Gospel of Jesus that transforms lives. Only through the death, burial, and resurrection of Christ does He save us from our sins.

The lack of biblical knowledge is a serious matter. It leads to people being held captive by Satan and being oppressed by devils. God's Word declares that *"where the Spirit of the Lord is, there is liberty"* (2 Corinthians 3:17).

If a man or woman is living in bondage they are not enjoying the fullness of the Christian life the Lord intended. Jesus said, *"If the Son therefore shall make you free, ye shall be free indeed"* (John 8:36).

In the book of Acts we don't read of saints attending deliverance meetings. Why? Because those new believers accepted the truth when God's Son proclaimed, *"I give the authority...over all the powers of the enemy, and nothing shall by any means hurt you"* (Luke 10:19, NKJV). Jesus wasn't speaking to the unsaved, but to you!"

I have seen Christians who are demon harassed and demon oppressed, but if Christ is truly in your heart you cannot be possessed by Satan. That's impossible because possession means ownership, and you can't belong to both Satan and Christ at the same time.

Jesus said, *"My sheep hear my voice"* (John 10:27). We are not the devil's sheep! *"Blessed (happy, fortunate, to be envied) is the nation whose God is the Lord, the people He has chosen as His heritage"* (Psalm 33:12, AMP). He has *"blessed us with all spiritual blessings"* (Ephesians 1:3). This doesn't sound like bondage to me!

CAN SATAN CONTROL YOU?

As you study the works of the devil, be forewarned —demons react. They will unleash their arrows to attack your thoughts and confuse your thinking. So expect it and be ready to respond in the name of Jesus.

Just because you are a Christian doesn't mean you are immune to the onslaughts of Satan. We fully understand that *"we wrestle not against flesh and blood, but against...the rulers of the darkness of this world"* (Ephesians 6:12). Satan is *"a roaring lion...seeking whom he may devour"* (1 Peter 5:8).

While that is true, we also know that if we are walking with the Lord, covered with the blood, and protected by the Holy Spirit, the devil cannot touch us! He may look through our window, but he will not be able to gain entrance. That line he cannot cross.

We have all been his target, but I can tell you that the day I gave my heart to the Lord, I was free! From the moment the anointing of God touched my life, I have not known a second of Satan's oppression, depression, or anything close.

The Bible promises this liberty to every believer! So I am puzzled when I see Christians who seem to be living under a black cloud or in spiritual bondage. I cannot help but ask myself, what is wrong with their salvation?

If you find yourself in this category, it's time to rise to the level of God's Word. The Lord can lift you out of your pit and place you back on the mountaintop where you belong.

A PERFECT WORLD?

As we look at demons, we cannot ignore what we discussed in chapter 5 concerning the fall of Lucifer.

We established the pre-Adamic dateless past when God created the heavens (the three mentioned in Scripture) and the earth (Genesis 1:1).

We talk about time and space, but our finite minds cannot comprehend when these didn't exist, but the Almighty knows. For this reason we can say God never *was*—He *is!*

What a great Jehovah! The Bible tells us, *"He is the Rock, his work is perfect"* (Deuteronomy 32:4). To be specific, *"God himself that formed the earth and made it; he hath established it, he created it not in vain, he formed it to be inhabited"* (Isaiah 45:18).

By this we know that God had an eternal purpose when He made this world. It was for us to live in. Furthermore, *"He hath made every thing beautiful"* (Ecclesiastes 3:11). Not only that, *"as for God, his way is perfect"* (Psalm 18:30).

It is clear from these passages that the earth God created was flawless, designed for a purpose, and was lovely to look upon. There are no defects in the works of the Almighty.

Yet, when we read Genesis 1:2, we find an earth that *"was without form, and void."*

Oh my! If the Bible tells us that everything God made was perfect and without fault, how can this be?

What was missing on this planet? Why was it void? It was empty, not a blade of grass, not a drop of water, and was totally black: *"Darkness was upon the face of the deep"* (Genesis 1:2). No sun was shining down upon this planet.

Then we learn that in this foreboding place, *"the Spirit of God moved on the face of the waters"* (verse 2). There is only one conclusion we can come to. The earth was a ball of formless ice—no shape, no beauty, no light.

Absolutely nothing happens until the Spirit of God moves. That is still true today. The Word of God is the result of the work of the Holy Spirit: *"The letter kills, the Spirit gives life"* (2 Corinthians 3:6, NKJV). And Jesus declares, *"The words that I speak unto you, they are spirit, and they are life"* (John 6:63).

After the Spirit of God moved on the waters, God said, *"Let there be light"* (Genesis 1:3). We cannot confess the Word without first having the prompting of the Spirit.

THE EARTH REBORN

It is impossible to understand demonology without comprehending what took place between verses 1 and 2 of Genesis 1. That is why I have emphasized it in chapter 5 and am adding additional information here. How could the world go from perfection to destruction—from a beautiful earth to one that was desolate?

When the Creator uttered the words, *"Let there be light,"* the word *let* is one of permission. This tells us that the light that shone previously (before the world turned dark and void), was once again brightly shining.

It took me years of study to conclude that the earth is not 6,000 years old but has been here billions of years—and this does not conflict with scripture. It also brings into focus the presence of demons on this planet.

When God began to restore the earth, it was without form, empty, frozen in space, and covered with water because of His judgment. Let's examine the facts according to Scripture.

In Job 38, God speaks of the *"foundations of the earth"* (verse 4) and the creation of angels *"when the morning stars sang together, and all the sons of God shouted for joy"* (verse 7). This was when God created the earth the first time and it was perfect. After that came divine judgment.

The Almighty asks, *"Or who shut up the sea with doors, when it brake forth, as if it had issued out of the womb?"* (verse 8).

God punished this planet with a flood—the waters gushed out as a woman giving birth to a child. This is a picture of a flood so massive that it surged from the belly of the earth itself. Then He caused the waters to "shut" or to freeze, to be sealed with a door that was totally closed.

It is obvious this took place before man was created because later in this same chapter we read: *"Who hath divided a watercourse for the overflowing of waters, or a way for the lightning of thunder; to cause it to rain on the earth, where no man is"* (Job 38:25-26).

This cannot be Noah's flood because there were humans mocking him at the time he was building the ark. But in this verse it speaks of a period when it rained and no man existed.

FROZEN ICE?

You may question the concept of the earth being frozen,

but keep reading: *"To satisfy the desolate and waste ground;
and to cause the bud of the tender herb to spring forth? Hath
the rain a father? or who hath begotten the drops of dew?
Out of whose womb came the ice? and the hoary frost of
heaven. Who hath gendered it? The waters are hid as with a
stone, and the face of the deep is frozen"* (verses 27-30).

The flood waters turned to ice. If you look at Genesis 1:2,
we find that *"darkness was on the face of the deep"* until the
Spirit of God moved *"on the face of the waters."* And then
we are told *"The face of the deep is frozen."*

The planet was so cold and frigid it was as hard as a rock:
"The waters are hid as with a stone" (Job 38:30).

Scripture has even more to say concerning this pre-Adamic
flood. The psalmist speaks of God, *"Who laid the foundations
of the earth, that it should not be removed for ever. Thou
coveredst it with the deep as with a garment: the waters stood
above the mountains. At thy rebuke they fled; at the voice of
thy thunder they hasted away"* (Psalm 104:5-7).

The waters in Noah's day did not know God's
reprimand—nor did the waters flee! Instead it took many
months for the waters to recede enough for the ark to be able
to settle on dry ground (Genesis 8:3-5). However, Psalm 104
speaks of an abrupt removal of water. The earth went from
flooded to frozen, an instantaneous change.

A VIOLENT SHAKING

God created a world of perfection (Genesis 1:1), then
chaos erupted (verse 2). But what brought about this
judgment? What caused this paradise called earth to become
such a barren, black, empty place?

Scripture describes a God so upset that He literally shook

the world: *"Which removeth the mountains, and they know not: which overturneth them in his anger. Which shaketh the earth out of her place, and the pillars thereof tremble. Which commandeth the sun, and it riseth not; and sealeth up the stars"* (Job 9:5-7).

According to the Bible, nothing like that has ever happened since the creation of man, nor will it take place after the coming of the Lord. Not even when God creates a brand new earth. Therefore this could only be pre-Adamic when there was darkness on the face of the deep (Genesis 1:2). That is when God commanded the sun not to rise and He sealed up the stars in the heavens (Job 9:7).

If God declared, "Let there be light," on the first day of the recreated earth, but the sun did not shine until day four (Genesis 1:14-19), what was the original light? It was God's awesome presence. And we know this because in John's revelation of the new heaven and new earth *"the city had no need for the sun, neither of the moon, to shine in it: for the glory of God did lighten it, and the Lamb is the light thereof"* (Revelation 21:23).

What an amazing day that will be!

ROTATION RESTORED

God's glorious presence brought the light in Genesis 1:3. Then He divided the light from darkness—the Creator *"called the light Day, and the darkness he called Night"* (verse 5).

Up until this point, the earth was not rotating. There was no sun, and our universe was frozen and at a standstill. Then God restored the rotation of our planet and ordered that there be *"firmament in the midst of the waters"* (Genesis 1:6). The ice melted so the earth was then covered with water that was no longer frozen.

The Creator separated the atmosphere and let the waters *"under the heaven"* (verse 9) be gathered together. Then dry land appeared. It already existed but was hidden beneath the flood waters.

The fact that God said, *"Let the earth bring forth grass, the herb yielding seed, and the fruit tree* (verse 11) is evidence that the seeds for these plants were already here, having been covered by the great flood.

Let us look at the words of the prophet Jeremiah. God showed him the beginning of time and he wrote, *"I beheld the earth, and, lo, it was without form, and void; and the heavens, and they had no light"* (Jeremiah 4:23). This is a picture of the destroyed earth of Genesis 1:2.

In Jeremiah's vision, he *"beheld the mountains, and, lo, they trembled, and all the hills moved lightly"* (Jeremiah 4:23). These words mirror what was mentioned earlier in Job 9. Then the prophet Jeremiah states, *"I beheld, and, lo, there was no man"* (Jeremiah 4:25). It's the same description we read in Job 38:26. Again, this describes the earth after the first flood.

What Jeremiah spoke of next may sound puzzling, but it is significant. *"All the birds of the heavens were fled. I beheld, and, lo, the fruitful place was a wilderness, and all the cities thereof were broken down at the presence of the LORD, and by his fierce anger"* (Jeremiah 4:25:26).

This confirms what God revealed to Isaiah: *"Behold, the LORD maketh the earth empty, and maketh it waste, and turneth it upside down, and scattereth abroad the inhabitants thereof"* (Isaiah 24:1), which could only have happened before the creation of Adam. Because the earth will not be turned upside down in the future, this had to be a pre-Adamic time of judgment.

WHO LIVED HERE?

This fertile land of plenty became a desolate wilderness with the destruction of the earth. It was an inverted, icy planet. The North Pole became the South Pole! The inhabitants were scattered near and far!

We read that the birds had fled and cities were destroyed, but who lived on this earth? What did they look like? What were their names? Where did they come from?

Summing up the biblical facts, I came to the conclusion that these inhabitants are the demons that are in our world today. They are here mingling with us, not in the millions, but in the billions!

You may think that demons are alien angels, but as we will learn later, that is not accurate. These are the same devils that made a man in Vancouver growl at me, and a man in Ontario slither like a snake. Demons are roaming throughout the earth at this very moment, controlling countless lives.

They inhabit millions of people, making a home in their bodies. I have often said that because they seek to indwell bodies, they even fly on planes without tickets and can't be detected by body scanners. They are nameless, and thousands of them can dwell in one person. I am firmly convinced they are the multitude Isaiah spoke of whose cities were destroyed (Isaiah 24:1).

Demons are disembodied spirits, which means at one time they possessed a body. Later we will see how Scripture describes them in great detail.

SEEKING A PRIVILEGED POSITION

In part I of this book, when we discussed the archangel Lucifer, we referred to Isaiah 14, which tells us how he was kicked out of heaven. "*How art thou cut down to the ground, which didst weaken the nations!*" (verse 12). What nations? The ones that existed under his rule before he invaded heaven.

Look carefully at these words: "*You have said in your heart: 'I will ascend into heaven, I will exalt my throne above the stars of God; I will also sit on the mount of the congregation on the farthest sides of the north; I will ascend above the heights of the clouds, I will be like the Most High'*" (verses 13-14, NKJV). The *mount* here is symbolic of God's government.

Where did he ascend from? The earth.

When Lucifer said he will lift his throne above the stars of God, it tells us he had a kingdom and was a king but craved authority higher than the angels (stars) of God.

It's also significant that he desired to sit on the north side of the mountain. This is prized territory. As David wrote, "*Great is the LORD, and greatly to be praised in the city of our God...Beautiful for situation, the joy of the whole earth, is Mount Zion on the sides of the north, the city of the great King*" (Psalm 48:1-3).

Heaven itself is in the north (Job 26:7), and this is where Satan longed to be.

After convincing those on earth that God was their enemy, an extremely jealous Lucifer invaded heaven. One-third of all angels were taken in by his deception and joined him. But Scripture records how they were eventually cast to the ground and God's wrath destroyed the earth over which he ruled.

That is what Jesus spoke of when He said, *"I beheld Satan as lightning fall from heaven"* (Luke 10:18).

STONES OF FIRE

Remember, Lucifer was one of the three most illustrious angels God ever created. He was wiser than Solomon and *"perfect in beauty"* (Ezekiel 28:13).

He was also the "anointed cherub" who covered the throne of God (verse 14). So Satan understands the anointing better than we do!

As both an archangel and a cherub, his assignment of protecting the throne was given to him by the Almighty: *"I have set thee so"* (verse 14).

In Ezekiel 1 we read of cherubim literally hovering around where the glory resided. As chief of the cherubs, Lucifer made certain no one came close to the Almighty.

We also know Lucifer was in the Garden of Eden prior to Adam (verse 13. It is important to understand that there was more than one Eden. The pre-Adamic garden which existed billions of years ago was Lucifer's throne room on earth. It was his domain.

In his earthly kingdom, his garments were made of precious stones of topaz, diamonds, onyx, jasper, sapphires, emerald, and gold (Ezekiel 28:13). He literally glistened as he walked around.

Even though Lucifer was a spirit being, he was adorned with these jewels. Plus, he had musical instruments built into him: *"The workmanship of thy tabrets and of thy pipes"* (verse 13).

In addition, as an archangel who ascended to heaven, Lucifer was told by God, *"You were on the holy mountain of God; you walked back and forth in the midst of fiery stones"* (verse 14, NKJV). This parallels the moment Moses and the elders *"saw the God of Israel: and there was under his feet as it were a paved work of a sapphire stone"* (Exodus 24:10).

The very sight of the glory of the Lord *"was like devouring fire on the top of the mount"* in the eyes of the children of Israel (verse 17).

Daniel also saw God's throne *"like the fiery flame"* (Daniel 7:9).

NO MORE WISDOM

So Lucifer had the authority to walk up and down in the midst of the stones of fire, protecting the throne. According to Scripture he was perfect from the day he was created until *"iniquity was found in thee"* (Ezekiel 28:15).

Lucifer's transgression was this: *"By the multitude of thy merchandise they have filled the midst of thee with violence, and thou hast sinned"* (verse 16).

His assignment was to present God's law to the earth and its inhabitants, and to give the sacrifice of praise and the obedience of the earth back to God. What Lucifer did, however, was to retain the praise for himself instead of directing it toward the Almighty, and he prevented God's law from coming to the inhabitants of the earth. As such, he defiled God's law. He made "merchandise" of his position. In essence, Lucifer was saying, "I am God. Worship me!"

This was rebellion against a just and holy God, who said, *"Thine heart was lifted up because of thy beauty, thou hast corrupted thy wisdom by reason of thy brightness"* (Ezekiel 28:17).

Anyone who believes that the devil is still wise doesn't understand what took place when he was cast out of heaven. No, he is foolish. As the apostle Paul wrote, *"We speak the wisdom of God in a mystery, even the hidden wisdom, which God ordained before the world unto our glory: which none of the princes of this world knew: for had they known it, they would not have crucified the Lord of glory"* (1 Corinthians 2:7-8).

When the devil lost his wisdom, he also gave up his authority and possession. He has been a failure ever since. All his plans have gone astray, and he continues to make mistakes.

Another charge made against him was this: *"Thou hast defiled thy sanctuaries"* (verse 18), meaning he was a priest. We also know Lucifer was a king, since he bragged, *"I will exalt my throne above the stars of God"* (Isaiah 14:13).

The vanity of his beauty, wisdom, and perfection corrupted him.

A DESOLATE EARTH

Lucifer was responsible for giving God's Word to those who resided on the earth, and to direct the praise of those inhabitants back to God. He was to bridge the gap between earth and heaven, but he perverted his possession by vainly keeping the praise to himself and rebelling against God. He also made false charges against the Almighty. That is why Satan is called *"the accuser"* (Revelation 12:10).

Because of Lucifer's rebellion, the Almighty declared, *"I will cast thee to the ground"* (Ezekiel 28:17). The *ground* is the earth! And God added, *"I will bring thee to ashes upon the earth"* (verse 18).

In addition, the Lord told him He would do this *"in the sight of all them that behold thee. All they that know thee among the people shall be astonished at thee"* (verses 18-19). In other words, there were witnesses when Lucifer fell like lightening from heaven. No longer was he clothed in jewels or walking with music in his being. Now banished from heaven, he lost his perfection, beauty, and wisdom.

The earth Lucifer ruled over was decimated. The *"fruitful place"* became a wilderness (Jeremiah 4:26). God said, *"The whole land shall be desolate; yet will I not make a full end"* (verse 27). This speaks to the fact that the Lord would restore the earth at a later time.

The Almighty continued, *"For this shall the earth mourn, and the heavens above be black"* (verse 28). *This* refers to Lucifer's rebellion. The heavens above the earth became dark *"because I have spoken it, I have purposed it, and will not repent, neither will I turn back from it"* (verse 28).

Despite His Holy anger, which destroyed the earth, God was already making plans for its restoration.

A NEW EARTHLY KING

Envision Lucifer and his host of angels now living on a destroyed, formless earth. No longer were they welcome in heaven.

It was after this that God came to restore the earth as we read beginning with Genesis 1:3. However, since Satan and his angels and demons were still present, the Creator placed Adam in the Garden and let him know, "You are the new king!" God gave the first man and woman dominion over all that He had created (verse 26).

Cast out of heaven and no longer in charge, the devil was now powerless and inhabited the body of a serpent. Dismantled and defeated, he slithered up to Eve spewing this lie: *"Yea, hath God said, Ye shall not eat of every tree of the garden?"* (Genesis 3:1).

Eve told him there was one tree they were not allowed to eat from, the Tree of the Knowledge of Good and Evil. God had instructed Adam that if they touched or ate from this particular tree they would die (Genesis 2:17).

Satan responded with the greatest deception of all time: *"Ye shall not surely die: for God doth know that in the day ye eat thereof, then your eyes shall be opened, and ye shall be as gods, knowing good and evil"* (Genesis 3:4-5).

The deception worked. Both Adam and Eve gave into temptation and ate from the tree in their desire to be wise. They didn't realize they were already like God, because He had created them in His image.

At that moment, the devil recaptured the throne from Adam, the earthly king. The first man and woman suddenly became slaves to the former ruler of earth. The future seed of man was now under Satan's rule.

Think of the consequences! God created Adam after His image and His likeness—higher than angels. But the devil had taken authority.

When Satan recaptured the kingdom from Adam, he regained the earth (the first heaven) and established his domain in the second heaven, *"heavenly places"* (Ephesians 6:12). He certainly was not reigning there when the Lord threw him down to earth.

THE FIRST CURSE

When God was walking in the cool of the day, Adam and Eve *"hid themselves from the presence of the LORD God amongst the trees of the garden"* (Genesis 3:8). Living in sin because of eating the forbidden fruit, they were suddenly ashamed of their nakedness. Adam blamed Eve for their disobedience, and she blamed the serpent.

As a result, God placed a curse on Satan, telling him, *"Because thou hast done this, thou art cursed above all cattle, and above every beast of the field; upon thy belly shalt thou go, and dust shalt thou eat all the days of thy life: and I will put enmity between thee and the woman, and between thy seed and her seed; it shall bruise thy head, and thou shalt bruise his heel"* (verses 14-15).

In these words we find the promise of redemption that would one day come through the virgin birth of God's Son, Jesus Christ. The Savior was to be born through a woman (Mary), not by the seed of an earthly man.

When God told the devil that this seed would bruise his head, Satan initiated a new plan. He said, "I'll keep her seed from ever producing." What was his scheme?

We will discuss his plot in the next chapter.

CHAPTER 9

GIANTS IN THE LAND

W hat was the devil's devious strategy?

In Genesis 6 we discover that *"when men began to multiply on the face of the earth, and daughters were born unto them, that the sons of God saw the daughters of men that they were fair; and they took them wives of all which they chose"* (verses 1-2).

The "sons of God" in scripture refers to angels. This is evident when we read, *"There were giants in the earth in those days; and also after that, when the sons of God came in unto the daughters of men, and they bare children to them, the same became mighty men which were of old, men of renown"* (verse 4).

As strange as it sounds, fallen angels were fathering giants!

It was following this that God saw the overwhelming wickedness on earth and how the thoughts of men were continually evil. This is when *"it repented the Lord that he had made man on the earth, and it grieved him at his heart. And the LORD said, I will destroy man whom I have created from the face of the earth"* (Genesis 6:6-7).

The fact that God said He would destroy man and not the earth is worth noting. Remember, in the first flood, the earth was destroyed, in the second, man was destroyed.

Satan's ploy to prevent the seed of the woman from birthing God's Son was to cause wicked angels to sleep with women and infiltrate mankind with a combination of both the human and the angelic. I believe the reason God sent the second flood is because the earth was contaminated by wicked angelic seed.

There was only one man living on earth still carrying the pure Adamic seed: Noah. That is why Scripture records, *"Noah was a just man and perfect in his generations, and Noah walked with God"* (Genesis 6:9).

Think about it! Even though Noah's wife and sons were allowed to go with him into the ark, God's promise was only to Noah: *"With thee will I establish my covenant"* (verse 18).

Even his sons were corrupted, because giants existed after the flood and remained until the reign of King David. Goliath was a descendant of these giants.

The Bible also tells us about *"a battle in Gath, where was a man of great stature, that had on every hand six fingers, and on every foot six toes, four and twenty in number; and he also was born to the giant"* (2 Samuel 21:20). Eventually, the giants were eradicated from the land and their seed removed from the human race.

"STRANGE FLESH"

When I speak of angels being able to reproduce, you may wonder, "Is that in the Bible?"

According to the book of Jude, *"The angels which kept not their first estate, but left their own habitation, he hath reserved in everlasting chains under darkness unto the judgment of the great day. Even as Sodom and Gomorrah, and the cities about them in like manner, giving themselves over to fornication, and going after strange flesh, are set forth for an example, suffering the vengeance of eternal fire"* (Jude 6-7).

Here, the angels left their dwelling place and, duplicating what occurred at Sodom and Gomorrah, went after "strange flesh." This means they slept with women!

Scripture records, *"God spared not the angels that sinned, but cast them down to hell, and delivered them into chains of darkness, to be reserved unto judgment; and spared not the old world, but saved Noah the eighth person, a preacher of righteousness, bringing in the flood upon the world of the ungodly"* (2 Peter 2:4-5).

Again we see the connection between angels sinning with women, resulting in the flood of Noah's day. These angels, who were guilty of iniquity, were placed into an underworld, which brings us closer to the question: where do demons come from?

THE FIVE WORLDS BENEATH US

I believe that demons are the pre-Adamic race that at one time inhabited the earth under Lucifer's rule. After his fall from heaven, these demons were placed in a pit, which is still their world today. But before going deeper into this, let's examine the underworld itself.

There is a familiar passage in the New Testament that contains a fact many people overlook: *"Wherefore God also hath highly exalted him, and given him a name which is above every name: that at the name of Jesus every knee should bow, of things in heaven, and things in earth, and things under the earth; and that every tongue should confess that Jesus Christ is Lord, to the glory of God the Father"* (Philippians 2:9-11).

This speaks of what will eventually happen everywhere, including "under the earth," in the underworld. Every being is to confess Christ. This includes billions of people—in heaven, on earth, and under the earth.

My study of Scripture leads me to conclude that there are five worlds beneath us. Let's examine them:

1. Hell

The Hebrew word for "hell" is *sheol,* and we find it included in several verses.

"A fire is kindled in mine anger, and shall burn unto the lowest hell [sheol]" (Deuteronomy 32:22). *"I shall go to the gates of the grave [sheol]"* (Isaiah 38:10.) *"They spend their days in wealth, and in a moment go down to the grave [sheol]"* (Job 21:13).

Hell is a world, with countless inhabitants, that still exists. Those sentenced to this place of torment don't linger around after death. They go there instantly, *"in a moment"* (see also Psalm 73:19).

2. Paradise

I believe this second world is part of hell itself today.

After His death at Calvary, Christ *"first descended into the lower parts of the earth"* (Ephesians 4:7) to set captivity free, and then ascended on high *"that he might fulfill all things"* (verse 10).

The story of the rich man and Lazarus also gives us an insight into this place.

Jesus shared the account of a wealthy man who dressed expensively and wasted his days spending money like there was no tomorrow. However, at his doorstep was a poor man named Lazarus who was covered with sores and eked out a meager existence eating the scraps from the rich man's table.

One day *"the beggar died, and was carried by the angels into Abraham's bosom"* (Luke 16:22). Abraham's bosom is a term for paradise.

We also learn that the rich man died and was buried — *"and in hell he lifted up his eyes, being in torments, and seeth Abraham afar off, and Lazarus in his bosom"* (verse 23).

Two distinct destinations are mentioned here: paradise (where the beggar went) and hell (where the wealthy man was sent).

In this horrible place, the rich man was able to see to the other side because it said he *"seeth Abraham afar off, and Lazarus in his bosom"* (verse 23). We also discover that in hell people can talk, pray, and know what is going on around them, because the wealthy man cried out, *"Father Abraham, have mercy on me, and send Lazarus, that he may dip the tip of his finger in water, and cool my tongue; for I am tormented in this flame"* (verse 24).

Abraham reminded the man of means that during his time on earth he enjoyed the good things of life, while Lazarus endured the bad. But now the tables were turned: *"He is comforted, and thou art tormented. And beside all this, between us and you there is a great gulf fixed: so that they which would pass from hence to you cannot; neither can they pass to us, that would come from thence"* (Luke 16:25-26).

At that point the rich man begged Abraham to send someone to warn his five brothers to change their ways so they wouldn't end up in hell. Abraham told him, *"'They have Moses and the prophets; let them hear them.' And he said, 'No, father Abraham; but if one goes to them from the dead, they will repent.' But he said to him, 'If they do not hear Moses and the prophets, neither will they be persuaded though one rise from the dead'"* (verses 29-31, NKJV).

Today, paradise is empty and has become a part of hell. Scripture says, *"Hell hath enlarged herself"* (Isaiah 5:14).

The Bible tells us that the moment Jesus died on the cross *"the veil of the temple was rent in twain from the top to the bottom; and the earth did quake, and the rocks rent"* (Matthew 27:51).

We know that Jesus spent at least three days in paradise, because He told the thief on the cross He would meet him there (Luke 23:43).

After Christ came out of the tomb, all the saints that were in paradise rose with Him: *"The graves were opened; and many bodies of the saints which slept arose, and came out of the graves after his resurrection, and went into the holy city [Jerusalem], and appeared unto many"* (Matthew 27:51-53). Hallelujah!

Imagine the joy and excitement when countless Old Covenant saints rose from the dead to greet their families on the way to heaven.

On that day, untold millions were lifted out of paradise.

3. Tartarus

In a verse we mentioned earlier, God cast the angels that sinned *"down to hell, and delivered them into chains of darkness"* (2 Peter 2:4). "Hell" in the Greek here is *tartarus,* meaning "prison."

These are the same angels found in Jude 6-7 and the ones

Jesus preached to. *"For Christ...being put to death in the flesh, but quickened by the [Holy] Spirit: by which also he went and preached unto the spirits in prison [tartarus]; which sometime were disobedient, when once the longsuffering of God waited in the days of Noah"* (1 Peter 3:18-20). Notice the connection with the second flood: *"While the ark was being prepared, in which a few, that is, eight souls, were saved through water"* (verse 20, NKJV).

Since living beings are never called "spirits" in the Bible, just men, I believe Jesus went to preach to a group of angels who were disobedient and slept with women at the time of the flood—the ones who obeyed Satan and his attempt to block Christ's coming to earth.

Jesus descended into paradise to release the saints, but He went to *tartarus* to announce His victory.

4. The Pit

The habitation of demons is called "the pit."

When Jesus cast the demons out of the man in Gadarenes, the one they couldn't hold down with chains, the devils begged the Lord not to send them *"out into the deep"* (Luke 8:31), or the pit.

The demons said they would rather be sent into some pigs nearby. So that's what Jesus did, and the animals ran off a cliff and were drowned in the sea.

I have been asked, "How are demons loosed? How are they released from the pit?"

It happens because people's desire for them on earth draws them out. Today, millions of demons exist on the earth and seek individuals they can reside in.

After the Rapture, the day will come when wickedness will be so rampant that virtually all demons will be loosed from the pit. There is a picture of this in Revelation 9, where an angel is given the key to the bottomless pit. As he opens the door, out of the smoke appears what looks like locusts (Revelation 9:3). But that's just the beginning. The description of these demons is unlike anything we can imagine.

The shape of the locusts is *"like horses prepared for battle. On their heads were crowns of something like gold, and their faces were like the faces of men. They had hair like women's hair, and their teeth were like lions' teeth. And they had breastplates like breastplates of iron, and the sound of their wings was like the sound of chariots with many horses running into battle. They had tails like scorpions, and there were stings in their tails"* (Revelation 9:7-10, NKJV).

I don't know what demons looked like prior to Adam, but according to this account the demons that will be released during the great Tribulation will be a mix of animal and man. At that time there will be such torment that *"men will seek death and will not find it; they will desire to die, and death will flee from them"* (verse 6, NKJV).

Thank God, you and I will be raptured before that dreadful day.

5. Gehenna

The fifth underworld is Gehenna, the lake of fire and future home of the antichrist, sinful men and women, and all wicked angels. This will be the home of Satan forever.

Gehenna is described as a place of *"everlasting fire, prepared for the devil and his angels"* (Matthew 25:41), where the *"worm shall not die, neither shall their fire be quenched"* (Isaiah 24).

The lake of fire is not a body of water as we know it, but a world unto itself. It will be the abode of untold numbers of human beings!

It is impossible for us to grasp how massive the world below us is. The Bible tells us that *"death and hell were cast into the lake of fire"* (Revelation 20:14).

One thing is for sure: because we have been redeemed by the blood of the Lamb, we are not going there. Our home is heaven, because of God's amazing grace!

YOUR AUTHORITY OVER DEMONS

When we talk about evil angels fathering giants, demonic activity, and the underworld, it is easy to become fearful and afraid. So before we delve deeper into this study, I want you to know that as a born again believer you have power over the devil and all of his demons.

Satan has been called a lion (1 Peter 5:8), a serpent (Revelation 12:9), and a dragon (verse 13); but God declares, *"Thou shalt tread upon the lion and adder: the young lion and the dragon shalt thou trample under feet"* (Psalm 91:13).

You can depend upon this because Jesus, God's Son, gave us His word and promise: *"I give you the authority...over all the power of the enemy, and nothing shall by any means hurt you"* (Luke 10:19, NKJV).

Stand on the promises of God: *"Unto you that fear my name shall the Sun of righteousness arise with healing in his wings; and ye shall go forth...And ye shall tread down the wicked; for they shall be ashes under the soles of your feet"* (Malachi 4:2-3).

The key to your victory is found in the first six words: "Unto you that fear my name." If you revere, respect, and fear God, you'll never have to worry about the devil.

Understanding who you are in Christ gives you the authority to command Satan to flee (Mark 16:17). And remember, *"greater is he that is in you, than he that is in the world"* (1 John 4:4).

It's time to send the devil packing!

CHAPTER 10

BEWARE OF THE GREAT DECEIVER

In your study of demons and deliverance, always stay within the borders of the Bible and let scripture be your source of reference—nothing else. Even if it's a popular bestseller, do not be tempted to read a book dealing with spirits written by an unbeliever.

We are commanded by God to *"neither give place to the devil"* (Ephesians 4:27). Even though we need knowledge from the Word of God regarding where Satan comes from and how he operates, we simply cannot give him access to our lives.

Followers of Christ love to quote the scripture, *"Resist the devil, and he will flee from you"* (James 4:7), but many are unsure how to go about the process. But the first part of the same verse tells us exactly what to do: *"Submit yourselves therefore to God"* (verse 7).

We don't scare the devil by simply shouting, "I resist you. I resist you!" We withstand his influence by totally yielding our lives to the Lord and His authority. So instead of wasting your time searching for the enemy, turn your heart, mind, and soul over to God and rest in His protection.

As you read the New Testament, you won't find Jesus or the apostles looking for Satan behind every rock, but when he reared his ugly head, they certainly knew how to stand against him.

Today, we resist the enemy by exercising our faith: *"Be sober, be vigilant; because your adversary the devil, as a roaring lion, walketh about, seeking whom he may devour: whom resist steadfast in the faith, knowing that the same afflictions are accomplished in your brethren that are in the world"* (1 Peter 5:8-9).

The devil preys upon men and women who are spiritually anemic—not submitted to the Lord and are lacking faith and trust in God. That is why you must daily fortify your faith.

YOU ARE THE GUARDIAN

I pray you will make a covenant with God that you will not knowingly associate with any part of Satan's kingdom. That includes not reading fiction or watching movies that contain themes of witchcraft, sorcery, and New Age subject matter.

We must take our role as parents seriously, including screening the cartoons our children watch. What may seem harmless can expose them to an underworld that should be avoided. Certain videos may be fun to play, but young people can quickly find themselves role-playing or pretending they are occult characters. Some music presents the same kind of devices. I have been a guest in Christian homes where satanic symbols were emblazoned on music CD covers that their teens were listening to.

Why open the door and allow entrance to the devil?

Years ago, there was a woman who found Christ in the church I pastored in Florida. She was a bright, outgoing, married mother. On Friday nights, however, she enjoyed watching midnight scary movies with storylines of witches and devils.

It wasn't long until demonic thoughts began to attack her mind and she became one of the most miserable, oppressed individuals I had ever seen.

Even as a godly person, when you flirt with the devil you are playing with fire. He is not seeking a friend but a man or woman *"he may devour"* (1 Peter 5:8). These words were not written to the unsaved, but as a warning to believers! The devil is not out to destroy his own family; his objective is to devour God's children.

That is why Satan is a master at infiltrating the media, attempting to penetrate the thinking of weak Christians with innocent-looking materials that contain a deadly message.

KEEP THE DEMONS OUT!

I was born and raised in a part of the world that is filled with demonic activity.

When we were kids, before I became a born again believer, fortune-tellers often stopped by our home to read palms, tea leaves, or whatever. Our family accepted it as a normal part of the culture.

Recently, I was talking with a group of Christians from Egypt, and they shared with me that in one area of Cairo, demon activity is so prevalent that they actually saw soda bottles lifted from the streets, floating in mid-air!

Even if you are not personally involved with people who are demonic, if you allow objects into your home connected with the occult, you bring devils with them. Demons can attach themselves to art, books, and any number of physical items. Even a painting hanging on your wall could contain elements connected to a world you want nothing to do with.

I tell believers that when they buy a home where someone else has lived, take the time to walk through every room and apply the blood of Jesus, whether the devil has been there or not.

Demons love to return to a place they once lived. As Jesus tells us, *"When an unclean spirit goes out of a man, he goes through dry places, seeking rest, and finds none. Then he says, 'I will return to my house from which I came.' And when he comes, he finds it empty, swept, and put in order. Then he goes and takes with him seven other spirits more wicked than himself, and they enter and dwell there; and the last state of that man is worse than the first"* (Matthew 12:43-45, NKJV).

The Lord is warning us not to leave our lives unprotected from evil forces. We need to sweep our house clean and invite Christ to take up permanent residence.

AVOID GOD'S WRATH

In preparation for the long awaited day when the children of Israel would enter into the Promised Land, God gave this stern word of caution:

If you hear someone in one of your cities, which the LORD your God gives you to dwell in, saying, "Corrupt men have gone out from among you and enticed the inhabitants of their city, saying, 'Let us go and serve other gods'"—which you have not known —then you shall inquire, search out, and ask diligently. And if it is indeed true and certain that such an abomination was committed among you, you shall surely strike the inhabitants of that city with the edge of the sword, utterly destroying it, all that is in it and its livestock—with the edge of the sword. And you shall gather all its plunder into the middle of the street, and completely burn with fire the city and all its plunder, for the LORD your God. It shall be a heap forever; it shall not be built again. So none of the accursed things shall remain in your hand, that the LORD may turn from the fierceness of His anger and show you mercy, have compassion on you and multiply you, just as He swore to your fathers, because you have listened to the voice of the LORD your God (Deuteronomy 13:12-18, NKJV).

God Almighty didn't just tell us to destroy what is cursed, He demands, "Don't let these things remain in your hand. Never touch them again." We are to be completely set apart and free from any objects or practices reviled by God.

This means we are to totally stay clear of people who practice any form of witchcraft. Don't even drink a cup of coffee with them. According to Scripture, *"Regard not them that have familiar spirits, neither seek after wizards, to be defiled by them: I am the LORD your God"* (Leviticus 19:31). Notice how our heavenly Father puts His signature at the end of this verse to seal it.

Unless you want the wrath of God to fall on you, keep your distance from the works of the devil. The Lord warns, *"The person who turns to mediums and familiar spirits, to prostitute himself with them, I will set My face against that person and cut him off from his people"* (Leviticus 20:6, NKJV).

Obeying God's directive is vital for your protection and safety as a believer.

STAND BLAMELESS

Again and again the Lord forewarned the children of Israel that when they entered their new land they should not follow the abominations of the inhabitants. Specifically, *"There shall not be found among you any one that maketh his son or his daughter to pass through the fire, or that useth divination, or an observer of times, or an enchanter, or a witch. Or a charmer, or a consulter with familiar spirits, or a wizard, or a necromancer"* (Deuteronomy 18:10-11).

The term "pass through the fire" refers to the practice of child sacrifice in order to appease a pagan god, but it also applies to burning incense in the belief it will drive devils away.

God also tells us to keep our distance from those who use horoscopes (an observer of times), cast spells (a charmer), or seek answers from the dead (a necromancer).

We are to stand blameless before Him.

NEVER TOUCH WHAT IS CURSED

Be aware that there are consequences for touching what is cursed. Think of what took place during the time of Joshua after his great victory at the battle of Jericho.

The children of Israel were fired up, ready to possess the land. The next city to be conquered was Ai. Those who went to spy out the territory returned with the news: "Don't bother sending a great army. The population is sparse—two or three thousand men should easily do the job."

However, when the army reached the city gates, the men of Ai were ready and waiting with an ambush. Thirty-six of Joshua's men were killed and the remainder fled in defeat (Joshua 7:5). This was quite an emotional letdown after their successful conquest of Jericho, where they didn't lose one man.

In anguish, Joshua tore his clothes, fell on his face before the Ark of the Lord, and cried, *"GOD, why have You brought this people over the Jordan at all—to deliver us into the hand of the Amorites, to destroy us?"* (verse 7, NKJV).

God did not mince His words telling Joshua exactly what the problem was. *"Get up! Why do you lie thus on your face? Israel has sinned, and they have also transgressed My covenant which I commanded them. For they have even taken some of the accursed things, and have both stolen and deceived; and they have also put it among their own stuff"* (Joshua 7:10-11 NKV).

They knew the divine rules. Previously, God had warned that if any man looted a cursed item from Jericho, all of Israel would suffer (Joshua 6:18). But they didn't listen to His words.

Until they destroyed those cursed, stolen objects, the Lord said He would turn His back on Israel. So the next morning Joshua called the people to gather before him, tribe by tribe.

Finally, he singled out a man named Achan from the tribe of Judah, who confessed, *"I have sinned against the LORD God of Israel"* (Joshua 7:20), and he admitted how he coveted and plundered a beautiful robe, 200 shekels of silver, plus a large gold bar, and hid them in his tent.

Evidently these items contained engravings or art that represented the devil, and God called them cursed. Only after Achan, his family, and all his possessions were brought before the people and destroyed did victory return to the camp of Israel.

What a chilling lesson for those who are tempted to touch the devil's "stuff"!

WHAT YOU SHOULD KNOW ABOUT THE DEVIL

In order to stand strong and resist the great deceiver, we need to learn all we can about his origin, plans, personality, and purpose. What is he like, and what does he do?

Here are 20 facts you need to know about Satan:

1. The devil was created by God.

We must always remember that everything made by the Almighty was pure perfection, and that includes the devil. Before Lucifer was cast out of heaven, God said to him, *"Thou wast perfect in thy ways from the day that thou wast created"* (Ezekiel 28:12). Paul later wrote, *"By him were all things created, that are in heaven, and that are in earth, visible and invisible, whether they be thrones, or dominions, or principalities, or powers: all things were created by him"* (Colossians 1:16).

2. The devil was the first ruler of the earth.

Yes, Satan was banished from heaven, but long before that

time, he ruled this planet. Earth was his kingdom. In Isaiah, the devil bragged, *"I will ascend into heaven, I will exalt my throne above the stars of God"* (Isaiah 14:13).

3. The devil has been seen with a physical body.

Most people have a mental image of the devil with horns and a tail and holding a pitchfork. I think we've seen too many Halloween costumes! It is recorded that when the devil appeared on the Mount of Temptation, he had a human-like physical body and walked and talked with Jesus (Matthew 4:1-11).

In John's revelation, he saw an angel take hold of the devil and bind his body with chains (Revelation 20:1-3).

4. The devil has a heart.

We know from God's Word that Satan has an "inner man" that feels emotion and makes decisions. In describing the devil's determination to challenge the Almighty, we read, *"Thou hast said in thine heart...I will exalt my throne above the stars of God"* (Isaiah 14:13). He wanted to be like the Almighty.

5. The devil is full of pride.

It's been said that pride goes before a fall, and this was certainly true in the case of Lucifer. Scripture vividly tells of the devil's self-admiration and conceit: *"Thine heart was lifted up because of thy beauty, thou hast corrupted thy wisdom by reason of thy brightness"* (Ezekiel 28:17).

137

6. The devil has the ability to speak.

Just before Job's faith was severely tested, Satan approached God who posed the question to him: *"Have you considered My servant Job, that there is none like him on the earth, a blameless and upright man, one who fears God and shuns evil?"* (Job 1:8, NKJV).

Satan answered the Lord and said, *"Does Job fear God for nothing? Have You not made a hedge around him, around his household, and around all that he has on every side?"* (verses 9-10).

God, however, had the final word, and Satan had to flee from the presence of the Lord.

In the New Testament, the devil chided Jesus, *"If thou be the Son of God, command that these stones be made bread"* (Matthew 4:3).

7. The devil has power.

The might of the evil one will be evident in the Antichrist *"whose coming is after the working of Satan with all power and signs and lying wonders"* (2 Thessalonians 2:9). We also know that in the final battle of the ages, John saw a beast rise up *"and the dragon [Satan] gave him his power...and great authority"* (Revelation 13:2).

8. The devil has desires.

The enemy of your soul hungers and craves after certain objectives. At the Last Supper, Jesus said to Peter, *"Satan hath desired to have you, that he may sift you as wheat"* (Luke 22:31).

Nothing has changed through the centuries. The evil one is still on the prowl!

9. The devil has a dwelling place.

God told the church at Pergamos, *"I know your works, and where you dwell, where Satan's throne is...where Satan dwells"* (Revelation 2:13, NKJV).

Since the enemy's prime priority is to find a home in your heart, take the offensive and build a strong, spiritual barrier.

10. The devil rules and controls on earth.

In Ephesians 2:2, Satan is called *"the prince of the power of the air."* As such, he spreads his rebellion and evil into every corner of mankind, including family, business, social, political, and even religious life.

11. The devil has a kingdom.

At this very moment, Satan is still a king who rules over a kingdom.

During the early days of Jesus' earthly ministry, the religious leaders accused Him of using the power of the devil to cast out demons. But Jesus answered them with a thought-provoking question, *"How can Satan cast out Satan? If a kingdom is divided against itself, that kingdom cannot stand"* (Mark 23-24, NKJV).

12. The devil is a religious leader today.

It may come as a surprise, but Satan exerts spiritual

leadership on earth. Scripture describes how he disguises himself and *"is transformed into an angel of light. Therefore it is no great thing if his ministers also be transformed as the ministers of righteousness"* (2 Corinthians 11:14–15).

There is a definite distinction between being religious and being a born again child of God.

13. The devil is a deceiver.

From the beginning, when Satan told Eve that if she ate of the Tree of the Knowledge of Good and Evil she would *"not surely die"* (Genesis 3:4), every word that has flowed out of his mouth has been false: *"When he speaketh a lie, he speaketh of his own: for he is a liar, and the father of it"* (John 8:44).

We find this from Genesis to Revelation: *"That old serpent, called the Devil, and Satan, which deceiveth the whole world...was cast out into the earth"* (Revelation 12:9).

14. The devil tempts us.

When the Lord Jesus taught us how to pray, He included these words: *"Do not lead us into temptation, but deliver us from the evil one"* (Matthew 6:13, NKJV).

He knows first hand how talented Satan is in his attempts to trick us. He was led *"into the wilderness to be tempted of the devil"* (Matthew 4:1).

15. The devil provokes man to sin.

In Scripture we read how *"Satan stood up against Israel, and provoked David to number [or take a census of] Israel"*

(1 Chronicles 21:1). Substituting statistics for trust in the Almighty was totally against the Lord's desire. This is why David confessed to God, *"I have sinned greatly, because I have done this thing"* (verse 8).

16. The devil will enter into a union with men against God.

If Satan finds a man or woman who is in conflict with the Lord, he will join forces with that individual. Just before Jesus gave communion to His disciples, *"Satan entered Judas"* (Luke 22:3, NKJV). That was the beginning of the great betrayal.

17. The devil sends messengers to fight and defeat the saints.

The apostle Paul wrote to the believers at Corinth, *"Lest I should be exalted above measure through the abundance of the revelations, there was given to me a thorn in the flesh, the messenger of Satan to buffet me"* (2 Corinthians 12:7).

The purpose of Satan was to defeat this effective missionary evangelist, and he still assigns his evil agents to assault believers.

18. The devil opposes and hinders the Gospel.

To a man possessed by demons, Paul said, *"Thou child of the devil, thou enemy of all righteousness, wilt thou not cease to pervert the right ways of the Lord?"* (Acts 13:10).

One of Satan's additional objectives is to steal the Word from those who have heard the Gospel. Jesus explained,

"When anyone hears the word of the kingdom, and does not understand it, then the wicked one comes and snatches away what was sown in his heart" (Matthew 13:19, NKJV).

19. The devil sets traps for men.

Constantly, Satan is creating new ways to ensnare us. The Bible teaches that a Christian leader *"must have a good testimony among those who are outside [the church], lest he fall into reproach and the snare of the devil"* (1 Timothy 3:7).

Satan's objective is to steal, kill, and destroy, but Christ came to give us life *"more abundantly"* (John 10:10). Halellujah!

20. The devil will finally be defeated.

While on earth we must deal with a persistent adversary who is out to make war on the saints, but please don't be discouraged. I am happy to report that the day is coming when *"the devil that deceived them was cast into the lake of fire and brimstone...and shall be tormented day and night for ever and ever"* (Revelation 20:10).

That makes me want to shout!

CHAPTER 11

THE TWELVE SPIRITS

If you study the ministries of men and women used mightily of God, such as Smith Wigglesworth, William Branham, and Kathryin Kuhlman, you'll find they were keenly aware of the demon spirits that came against their work.

Most people view their difficulties as being a natural problem, not knowing how the devil attacks. As a result, they remain in bondage to the enemy.

Without question, I believe there are far more spirits active in this world than we are aware of. Let me share what the Bible has to say about the twelve leading spirits of the satanic world called the "strong men."

At the end of this chapter I will show you specifically how to overcome them.

Strong Man #1: A Jealous Spirit

Psychologists are quick to tell us that jealousy is a natural human emotion, but if you examine Scripture, you will discover that in most cases it is a demon.

During the journey of the children of Israel in the wilderness, the Lord spoke to Moses and asked him to tell the people what to do if a man's wife is unfaithful toward him: *"If the spirit of jealousy comes upon him and he becomes jealous of his wife...then the man shall bring his wife to the priest"* (Numbers 5:14-15, NKJV). There, he is to present *"a grain offering for jealousy"* (verse 15).

Even if *"she has not defiled herself"* (verse 14), yet the husband is jealous, the same rule applies.

There are two cases here regarding whether or not the wife has committed adultery, but if the man allows the spirit of jealousy to overtake him, the result is the same. The spirit of jealousy also manifests itself through other demon spirits, such as the spirit of suspicion, anger, rage, revenge, and even murder.

Proverbs 6:34-35 confirms that the spirit of jealousy brings with it the manifestations of other spirits: *"Jealousy is the rage of a man: therefore he will not spare in the day of vengeance. He will not regard any ransom; neither will he rest content, though thou givest many gifts."* A person with the spirit of jealousy will have no peace or contentment.

To come against this spirit, don't mistakenly call it rage or anger. Name it what it is—jealousy. Sometimes we are like boxers, flaying around, not knowing what we are hitting. We need to be like the apostle Paul who said, *"Therefore I run thus: not with uncertainty. Thus I fight: not as one who beats the air"* (1 Corinthians 9:26, NKJV).

When you boldly cast out the spirit of jealousy, you are freeing others from everything that goes with it.

Strong Man #2: A Lying Spirit

This has nothing to do with a child who tells a fib to their parents out of fear or some other form of pressure. That's simply human weakness, not a lying spirit. Not everybody who lies has a demon—otherwise all our children would be demon possessed.

The "lying spirit" we are discussing here always operates in conjunction with religion.

An example of this is found in the Old Testament when Ahab (the king of Israel) asked Jehoshaphat (king of Judah) to join forces with him to fight against the armies of Ramoth Gilead. Jehoshaphat agreed, but there was one requirement. He told Ahab, *"Please inquire for the word of the LORD today"* (2 Chronicles 18:4).

So Ahab gathered 400 of his prophets together and asked them if he should go to war. They gave enthusiastic approval. But Jehoshaphat persisted, *"Is there not still [one more] prophet of the LORD here, that we may inquire of Him?"* (verse 6).

Ahab admitted there was a prophet named Micaiah, *and said, "But I hate him, because he never prophesies good concerning me, but always evil"* (verse 8). Ahab's messengers called for Micaiah and encouraged him to be like the rest of the prophets who announced that Israel and Judah would be victorious in battle. But when Micaiah stood before the two kings, he said, *"As the LORD lives, whatever my God says, that I will speak"* (verse 13).

Concerning the upcoming conflict, Micaiah saw Israel scattered on the mountains as sheep with no shepherd. Then the prophet proclaimed: *"I saw the LORD sitting on His throne, and all the host of heaven standing on His right hand and His left. And the LORD said, 'Who will persuade Ahab king of Israel to go up, that he may fall at Ramoth Gilead?' So one spoke in this manner, and another spoke in that manner.*

Then a spirit came forward and stood before the LORD, and said, 'I will persuade him.' The LORD said to him, 'In what way?' So he said, 'I will go out and be a lying spirit in the mouth of all his prophets.' And the LORD said, 'You shall persuade him and also prevail; go out and do so.' Therefore look! The LORD has put a lying spirit in the mouth of these prophets of yours, and the LORD has declared disaster against you" (2 Chronicles 18:18-22).

How did the story end? Ahab believed the lying spirits and was killed in the battle.

This demon spirit manifests itself also as the spirit of adultery, the spirit of profanity, and the spirit of vanity. Jeremiah wrote, *"I have seen a horrible thing in the prophets of Jerusalem: they commit adultery and walk in lies; they also strengthen the hands of evildoers, so that no one turns back from his wickedness"* (Jeremiah 23:14, NKJV). Notice, they are religious men.

God says there is a curse on such people: *"Behold, I will feed them with wormwood, and make them drink the water of gall; for from the prophets of Jerusalem profaneness has gone out into all the land"* (verse 15).

This religious spirit produces vanity. *"Hearken not unto the words of the prophets that prophesy unto you: they make you vain: they speak a vision of their own heart, and not out of the mouth of the LORD"* (verse 16).

A lying spirit is also a superstitious spirit. *"For there shall be no more any vain vision nor flattering divination within the house of Israel"* (Ezekiel 12:24). This speaks of people who are into "signs" and superstition. The Bible tells us to stay away from such individuals.

Strong Man #3: A Familiar Spirit

King Saul once said to his servants, *"Seek me a woman that hath a familiar spirit, that I may go to her, and inquire of her. And his servants said to him, Behold, there is a woman that hath a familiar spirit at Endor"* (1 Samuel 28:7).

By inquiring of a witch, Saul separated himself from God and was soon killed in battle.

Seeking answers from a "familiar spirit" is forbidden by the Lord (Deuteronomy 18:10-12). As you study this spirit in the Bible, you'll find it manifests itself also as the spirits of astrology, horoscopes, fortune-telling, and the occult. As we discussed in chapter 10, have nothing to do with these things.

Strong Man #4: A Perverse Spirit

Never forget that a demon hides under different names. So in order to cast out a demon, you have to address it clearly. A nameless spirit is a hidden spirit. You find the name of the spirit by discerning the characteristics of the spirit you are dealing with.

There are ministers today who don't know what to do with people who are possessed! It is because they cannot discern which "strong man" is behind all this activity.

When Jesus confronted the demonic man at Gadarenes, He asked the demon, "What is your name?" (Luke 8:30).

Perversion is not just fornication; it deals with the spirit of error. Look at what Isaiah prophesied concerning the nation of Egypt. *"The LORD hath mingled a perverse spirit in the midst thereof: and they have caused Egypt to err in every work thereof, as a drunken man staggereth in his vomit. Neither shall there be any work for Egypt, which the head or tail, branch or rush, may do"* (Isaiah 19:14-15).

This perverse spirit caused an entire nation to live in error. And by saying, *"Neither shall there be any work,"* we discover it brings about laziness. Not all laziness is demonic, but there are certain people who never want to work; they would rather be fed than to feed. This spirit must be broken!

A perverse spirit hates God. As Scripture states, *"He that walketh in his uprightness feareth the LORD: but he that is perverse in his ways despiseth him"* (Proverbs 14:2). What a difference there is between a man who is righteous and one who is not! One fears God and the other hates Him.

This spirit also manifests itself in men who lust after women. We read, *"Thine eyes shall behold strange women, and thine heart shall utter perverse things"* (Proverbs 23:33). A man who never take his eyes off of a woman has a spirit of perversion. So if you say, "Devil, come out"—nothing happens. You must declare, "You devil of perversion. I cast you out!"

There is a perverse spirit behind those who continually speak things that are not biblical and are not able to discover the truth of God's Word. If you look closely, there is filth in their closet.

This spirit always twists the Word of God and will attempt to convince you the Bible doesn't say what it means. When the apostle Paul was preaching the Gospel in Cyprus, he confronted a false prophet who was determined to keep people from hearing the message of Christ. Under the anointing of the Holy Spirit, Paul looked at him and said, *"O full of all deceit and all fraud, you son of the devil, you enemy of all righteousness, will you not cease perverting the straight ways of the Lord? And now, indeed, the hand of the Lord is upon you, and you shall be blind, not seeing the sun*

148

for a time" (Acts 13:10-11, NKJV).

When you find such a spirit, call it by name and boldly come against it. God will do the rest.

Strong Man #5: The Spirit of Heaviness

God says He will give us *"the oil of joy for mourning [and] the garment of praise for the spirit of heaviness"* (Isaiah 61:3).

Such a spirit manifests itself as the spirit of grief, despair, hopelessness, rejection, self-pity, and gluttony. When you see a person who is always gloomy and depressed, never seeing the bright side of life, they are carrying the spirit of heaviness.

Yes, it is natural to grieve over the loss of a loved one, but sustained grief or despair over years is not of God. Hopelessness must never become a lifestyle. The Bible says that as believers we may be *"sorrowful, yet always rejoicing"* (2 Corinthians 6:10).

The word *heaviness* can also be applied to gluttony. There are individuals who cannot loose weight. They can be on pills and diets, but they keep on eating because a spirit of gluttony is dominating their life.

The reality of this spirit—whether grief, gloom, or gluttony must be dealt with.

Strong Man #6: The Spirit of Whoredom

The spirit of whoredom is one of the most evil, controlling spirits ever devised by Satan. As described by the prophet Hosea, *"My people ask counsel at their stocks, and their staff declareth unto them: for the spirit of whoredoms hath caused them to err, and they have gone a whoring from under their God. They sacrifice upon the tops of the mountains, and burn incense upon the hills"* (Hosea 4:12-13).

This spirit not only brings people into error, but as we see in this portion of Scripture, it manifests itself as the spirit of idol worship. Yes, it, too, is also a religious spirit.

Those involved in fornication and prostitution are never fully gratified. There is a demonic, inner urge that causes them to always seek more. *"You played the harlot with them and still were not satisfied"* (Ezekiel 16:28, NKJV). The spirit also affects your spiritual heart: *"How weak is thine heart!'" saith the LORD GOD, 'seeing thou doest all these things, the work of an imperious whorish woman'"* (verse 30).

Those possessed with this demon have no will of their own. When the spirit of whoredom seizes them, they can never say no to its urges—and will end up in some form of idolatry. They commit adultery because of a spirit of *"filthiness...and with all the idols of thy abominations"* (verse 32).

But here's the saddest part of all. The final result of being bound by this spirit is that the person ends up in poverty: *"They shall strip thee also of thy clothes, and shall take thy fair jewels, and leave thee naked and bare"* (verse 39). It devours their wealth.

Strong Man #7: The Spirit of Infirmity

One day Jesus was speaking in a synagogue, *"and behold, there was a woman who had a spirit of infirmity eighteen years, and was bent over and could in no way raise herself up"*(Luke 13:11, NKJV). What did Jesus do? He called her to Him and said, *"Woman, you are loosed from your infirmity"* (verse 12).

The Lord spoke directly to this spirit.

In the ministry God has so graciously allowed me to have, when I pray for the sick, I pray, "Lord, heal your people"; but when I detect the spirit of infirmity, I also command it in Jesus' name to leave.

Strong Man #8: A Deaf and Dumb Spirit

After the Lord came down from the Mount of Transfiguration, a large crowd gathered around Him. A man stepped forward and said, *"Master, I have brought unto thee my son, which hath a dumb spirit; and wheresoever he taketh him, he teareth him: and he foameth, and gnasheth with his teeth, and pineth away: and I spake to thy disciples that they should cast him out; and they could not"* (Mark 9:25).

As the story is recorded in the book of Matthew, the father, said, *"Lord, have mercy on my son: for he is lunatick, and sore vexed"* (Matthew 17:15). He was tormented by this devil.

A "dumb spirit" manifests itself as insanity. Plus, it is obvious that this child was having epileptic seizures. And by saying he was "pining away," it meant the boy didn't want to eat and was wasting away. When they brought the boy to Jesus, this *"spirit tare him; and he fell on the ground, and wallowed foaming"* (Mark 9:20).

The Lord asked the child's father how long this had been going on. It had been occurring since the boy was young. The distraught dad shared that *"ofttimes it [the demon] hath cast him into the fire, and into the waters, to destroy him: but if thou canst do any thing, have compassion on us, and help us"* (verse 22). In other words, the demon caused the boy to become suicidal.

That is when Jesus said to the father, *"If you can believe, all things are possible to him who believes"* (verse 23). And immediately the man cried out, *"Lord, I believe; help my unbelief!"* (verse 24).

Pay close attention to what the Lord said next. He rebuked the unclean spirit by saying to it, *"Thou deaf and dumb spirit, I command you, come out of him and enter him no more!"* (verse 25).

The boy was possessed, but the spirit itself was neither deaf nor dumb. Jesus wasn't speaking to the child, but to the demonic spirit that was in him. Scripture records, *"Then the spirit cried out, convulsed him [the child] greatly, and came out of him"* (verse 26).

Remember, the boy was insane, had epilepsy, and was suicidal, yet Jesus called the spirit "deaf and dumb." Why? Because the Lord knew the name of the demon that had possessed the boy, and cast that demon out. Therefore, a deaf and dumb spirit manifests itself as the spirit of insanity, epilepsy, and suicide.

Strong Man #9: The Spirit of Fear

When fear strikes, there is torment, terror, worry, timidity, and the feeling of being inferior. In fact, all phobias exist under this spirit, including the fear of heights or being afraid to go through a dark tunnel.

Those who are always sensing danger are bound by this spirit. The affects can include physical, uncontrollable trembling, and even nightmares. In the story of Job, we read, *"Fear came upon me, and trembling, which made all my bones to shake"* (Job 4:14).

God longs for His children to serve Him without fear,

because when this spirit leaves our life, the enemy will depart, too. The Lord's desire is *"that we being delivered out of the hand of our enemies might serve him without fear"* (Luke 1:74).

Without question, fear is the result of sin. If you go back to the beginning, after Adam and Eve listened to Satan and ate of the forbidden tree, they ran from the Lord. Then God called out to Adam and asked, *"Where art thou?"* (Genesis 3:9). Adam replied, *"I heard thy voice in the garden, and I was afraid, because I was naked; and I hid myself"* (verse 10).

The moment you allow sin to creep back into your life, fear also returns.

There are two kinds of fear: godly and satanic. Throughout Scripture we are commanded to fear the Lord, and this fear is the result of living right before God. It also motivates and moves you to do the will of the Almighty. For example, *"By faith Noah, being warned of God of things not seen as yet, moved with fear, prepared an ark to the saving of his house"* (Hebrews 11:7).

On the other hand, the satanic fear that comes because of sin will control your behavior. We read, *"There is no fear in love; but perfect love casteth out fear: because fear hath torment. He that feareth is not made perfect in love"* (1 John 4:18). So godly fear motivates, while satanic fear dominates.

What is the cure for fear, oppression, and terror? Righteousness: *"In righteousness shalt thou be established: thou shalt be far from oppression; for thou shalt not fear: and from terror; for it shall not come near thee"* (Isaiah 54:14).

Stand on the Word: *"God hath not given us the spirit of fear; but of power, and of love, and of a sound mind"* (2 Timothy 1:7).

Ask the Lord to deliver you from the spirit of fear.

Strong Man #10: The Spirit of Pride

Not all pride is bad. For instance, parents are proud of their children, and kids like to brag about their mom and dad. That's not a spirit—it is just normal! And as a follower of Christ, I take great pride in being a Christian.

The evil pride I am speaking of is one of arrogance, conceit, and egotism. That is what the Bible is speaking of here: *"Pride goeth before destruction, and an haughty spirit before a fall"* (Proverbs 16:18).

The manifestations of this causes a person to mock others and become stubborn—they feel they have all the answers and just won't listen to anyone. This spirit causes contention and fighting. *"By pride comes nothing but strife"* (Proverbs 13:10, NKJV). It also produces anger: *"Proud and haughty scorner is his name, who dealeth in proud wrath"* (Proverbs 21:24).

This self-righteous, controlling demon of pride is religious in nature—and man-centered rather than God-focused. Those who have this spirit often mock the Gospel.

If you detect this spirit, rebuke it in the name of Jesus.

Strong Man #11: The Spirit of Bondage

Yes, bondage is actually a spirit. As the apostle Paul wrote: *"Ye have not received the spirit of bondage again to fear"* (Romans 8:15). Notice that this spirit also often manifests itself in fear. It is important to discern which strongman you are dealing with.

Those who have the spirit of bondage are continually in anguish and torment. We read how *"Moses spake so unto the children of Israel: but they hearkened not unto Moses for anguish of spirit, and for cruel bondage"* (Exodus 6:9).

Far too often, people find themselves in bondage by choice. Every person who is addicted is bound by this spirit, whether it involves drugs, alcohol, tobacco, pornography, overeating, gambling, compulsive shopping, or other habits they cannot break.

Those bound by this spirit experience bitterness— bitterness against God, against parents, or any authority. It also results in spiritual blindness, and until they are broken from this they are unable to receive God's truth. They hear the Word but are not touched by it. You can witness to them, but it seems you are accomplishing nothing.

What is the answer? You must pray them out of this bondage, and in a moment I will show you how.

Strong Man #12: The Spirit of the Antichrist

You may ask, isn't the Antichrist a man? Yes, and one day he will rule on this earth for a short time. But there is also a spirit that is called the spirit of Antichrist. This spirit has nothing to do with the man himself!

This spirit has been on the earth for over 2,000 years: *"Every spirit that does not confess that Jesus Christ has come in the flesh is not of God. And this is the spirit of the Antichrist, which you have heard was coming, and is now already in the world"* (1 John 4:3, NKJV). It is here today!

What is this spirit of the Antichrist? How can we discern it? This spirit denies the virgin birth. There are churches and ministers today who deny that Jesus came to earth in the flesh.

This spirit also denies the deity of Christ. Some say He was

155

a prophet and a good man, but not that He is the Son of God. In addition, the spirit of the Antichrist denies that Christ died on the cross and rose from the dead. It is a spirit that exists primarily among the religious who acknowledge God, but they pray dead prayers and only believe certain parts of the Bible.

Sadly, the spirit of the Antichrist controls millions in our world.

A TURNING POINT

I was in Durban, South Africa, in 1982 at a meeting being conducted by evangelist Reinhardt Bonnke. I watched closely as he began to rebuke the spirit of infirmity. Then he became very specific: "I rebuke the devil of blindness! You devil of deafness, come out!" And he continued using this terminology as he prayed for those with cancer, arthritis, and other illnesses. People were being healed everywhere.

This was amazing to me. Even though I prayed for the sick in my own meetings, I never thought a blind person had a spirit that needed to be rebuked. I was just praying, "Lord, heal them." The only time I rebuked anything was when there was a physical manifestation of the devil's presence in a person.

When I returned to North America, I began rebuking illness, and suddenly the power of God was healing and delivering people as never before. This was prior to our crusades, when I was conducting services in various cities. About that time we began holding monthly healing meetings in Orlando and about 200 people would show up. But when I began rebuking sicknesses, the crowds rapidly grew to over 2,000. Why? Because miracles were taking place at an unprecedented rate. Our ministry exploded!

Later, at one of our crusades in North Carolina, the Lord told me to ask every deaf person to come to the front of the auditorium. At least 30 or 40 stepped forward. I stood on the platform and said, "You deaf spirit, I rebuke you in Jesus' name and command you to come out!"

Almost instantly, the ears of one after another began to pop open. Why? Because there was a demon behind their deafness and that spirit was broken.

EXERCISE YOUR AUTHORITY

I have learned to be extremely careful regarding how I come against problems. Otherwise I may be attempting to cast out a devil where none exists. And just the opposite, I could be ignoring a situation where there *is* a devil.

As Jesus ministered to people when He walked on earth, there were times He healed people where there was no demon spirit involved. For instance, on a Sabbath, as He entered the synagogue to teach, there was a man whose right hand was withered. In front of the scribes and Pharisees, Jesus told the man, *"Arise and stand here,"* (Luke 6:8, NKJV).

Then the Lord said, *"'Stretch out your hand.' And he did so, and his hand was restored as whole as the other"* (verse 10).

There was no casting out demons, just a simple word from the Master.

However, when there was a demonic spirit present, He confronted the devil and rebuked him before the healing took place. To the boy with uncontrollable seizures, *"Jesus rebuked the unclean spirit, and healed the child"* (Luke 9:42).

When Peter's mother-in-law had a great fever, Jesus

"stood over her, and rebuked the fever; and it left her" (Luke 4:39). It was a spirit that bound her, and Jesus cast it out.

Ask the Lord to give you guidance and discernment concerning the spirit you are dealing with.

As a believer, there is no need to fear the twelve demonic spirits we have discussed in this chapter. You have been given power and authority to rebuke them in the name of Jesus. Hallelujah!

CHAPTER 12

TAKE AWAY
THE DEVIL'S ARMOR

If you are ready to bind the "strong man" and defeat him once and for all, I want to show you how. First, however, you need to be fully aware of how demons operate—and seven devious methods they use to gain entrance into a life.

1. Demons enter through rebellion.

A rebellious spirit is the first step toward destruction.

Because of King Saul's disobedience against the law of God, the prophet Samuel had to tell him, *"Rebellion is as the sin of witchcraft, and stubbornness is as iniquity and idolatry. Because thou hast rejected the word of the LORD, he hath also rejected thee from being king"* (1 Samuel 15:23)

Because of rebellion *"the Spirit of the LORD departed from Saul, and an evil spirit from the LORD troubled him"* (1 Samuel 16:14). Saul went from liberty to being oppressed and harassed by demons.

Today, many children who rebel against their parents become drug addicts and sexual perverts. With rebellion comes hatred for authority, hatred toward self, and hatred toward God and His Word. Don't give Satan the opportunity to walk through this door.

2. Demons enter through abuse of the tongue.

You become open to demonic activity by what you say—your conversation and the language you use. The power of life and death is in the tongue.

Scripture tells us, *"He that keepeth his mouth keepeth his life: but he that openeth wide his lips shall have destruction"* (Proverbs 13:3). When your words are not wholesome, Satan finds a place to dwell. Even more, *"the wicked is snared by the transgression of his lips"* (Proverbs 12:13). Yes, you can become trapped by the abuse of your tongue. When people say things that cause harm to others, they dishonor God and invite demons in.

Since this is a two-way street, be careful what you allow people to tell you. Don't receive or respond to individuals who are living far from God. Words have consequences.

3. Demons enter through a critical spirit.

I'm sure you've met those who go through life tearing others down, dwelling on the negative, and seeking to find flaws rather than good. The apostle Paul asked, *"Why dost thou judge thy brother? or why dost thou set at nought thy brother? for we shall all stand before the judgment seat of Christ"* (Romans 14:10).

A condemning attitude brings destruction. God says,

"Whoever secretly slanders his neighbor, him I will destroy" (Psalm 101:5, NKJV). We are also instructed to *"shun profane and idle babblings, for they will increase to more ungodliness. And their message will spread like cancer"* (2 Timothy 2:16-17, NKJV).

Satan would like nothing more than to inflict you with the disease of a critical spirit.

4. Demons enter through fear.

We have already discussed how fear is one of the twelve demonic spirits called "strong man," but we must understand that is just an opening Satan uses to control your life. The reason it is used by the devil is because *"fear hath torment [and] he that feareth is not made perfect in love"* (1 John 4:18).

When fear strikes it can be devastating, often resulting in panic attacks and uncontrollable behavior. Perhaps you know someone who has had such an experience. If not conquered, their strength begins to wear away until they are helpless. It's all because of this powerful tool used by the devil.

Fear is demonic to the core and will attack without warning. That is why we have to stand on God's Word and fight its entrance. Say with the psalmist, *"The LORD is my light and my salvation; whom shall I fear? the LORD is the strength of my life; of whom shall I be afraid? When the wicked, even mine enemies and my foes, came upon me to eat up my flesh, they stumbled and fell. Though an host should encamp against me, my heart shall not fear: though war should rise against me, in this will I be confident"* (Psalm 27:1-3).

This is not the time to be afraid.

5. Demons enter through laziness.

There is a curse on the person who is lethargic, lifeless, and has no desire to work. That is why God tells us to flee from such behavior. God's Word counsels that *"the way of the slothful man is as an hedge of thorns"* (Proverbs 15:19).

It's been said that idle hands are the devil's workshop, and that's so. When there is laziness, Satan takes over.

The Lord is asking, *"How long will you slumber, O sluggard? When will you rise from your sleep? A little sleep, a little slumber, A little folding of the hands to sleep—so shall your poverty come on you like a prowler"* (Proverbs 6:9-11, NKJV). That prowler is the devil himself, seeking whom he may devour.

Remember, *"He becometh poor that dealeth with a slack hand: but the hand of the diligent maketh rich"* (Proverbs 10:4).

6. Demons enter through abnormal sexual activity.

Satan becomes extremely active in the person who rejects God's truth, and it intensifies in those who practice sexual behaviors that is not normal.

Scripture is specific regarding this matter. The Lord's wrath turned on those *"who exchanged the truth of God for the lie, and worshiped and served the creature rather than the Creator"* (Romans 1:25, NKJV). God gave them up *"to vile passions. For even their women exchanged the natural use for what is against nature. Likewise also the men, leaving the natural use of the woman, burned in their lust for one another, men with men committing what is shameful, and receiving in themselves the penalty of their error which was due"* (Romans 1:26).

By shunning God Almighty, they became filled with *"sexual immorality [and] evil-mindedness"* (verse 29).

Turn away from Satan's sexual perversion. *"Marriage is honourable in all, and the bed undefiled: but whoremongers and adulterers God will judge"* (Hebrews 13:4).

Never step beyond the borders of scripture.

7. Demons enter through the mixing of flesh and spirit.

In the natural world, there are consequences to mixtures. For example, when the seed of a horse is mixed with a donkey you have a mule, which is sterile and can't reproduce. In the spiritual world there are also dangers of mixing righteousness with wickedness. We are commanded, *"Be ye not unequally yoked together with unbelievers: for what fellowship hath righteousness with unrighteousness? And what communion hath light with darkness?"* (2 Corinthians 6:14).

My friend, you can't live for the world six days a week and live for God on Sunday. It doesn't work. That is why the Lord says, *"Wherefore come out from among them, and be ye separate, saith the Lord, and touch not the unclean thing; and I will receive you"* (verse 17).

Again, why open the door to demonic activity?

READY FOR BATTLE

God wants you, as a believer, to engage in a battle to destroy Satan's influence. However, an uninformed army is an army in peril. Sadly, some people are not prepared or armed for spiritual warfare, and they rush naked into battle. When they do, they sign their own death certificate.

We have been talking about the strong men of the devil, but we will never defeat them without the proper armor, the right information, and the ultimate protection. It is futile to make a move until we are clothed for the fight. If we are handicapped by the activities of the enemy we cannot function in God's army or defeat the devil.

Jesus addressed this issue directly. He said, *"If I cast out demons with the finger of God, surely the kingdom of God has come upon you"* (Luke 11:20, NKJV). To bind the strong man you need "the finger of God," the power of the Holy Spirit. Notice that Jesus used the term *"come upon you,"* not *unto* you. He also said the same words concerning the coming of the Holy Spirit: *"Ye shall receive power, after that the Holy Ghost is come upon you"* (Acts 1:8). "Upon you" deals with the power of God. So in order to bring deliverance to the captives, we must be clothed with the power of the Spirit.

Jesus continued, *"When a strong man, fully armed, guards his own palace, his goods are in peace. But when a stronger than he comes upon him and overcomes him, he takes from him all his armor in which he trusted, and divides his spoils"* (Luke 11:21-23, NKJV).

The "strong man" in this passage, of course, is Satan, and Jesus tells us this man is armed.

In this portion of Scripture, the Lord tells us exactly what is necessary to overcome and destroy the enemy. We begin by overcoming the strong man with strength, and the most powerful force always wins. That is why Jesus says we are to come against the devil being *"stronger than he"* (verse 23).

God's Word declares we are to *"be strong in the Lord, and in the power of his might"* (Ephesians 6:10). What is the source of your strength? Jesus tells us, *"Behold, I give unto you power...over all the power of the enemy: and nothing shall by any means hurt you"* (Luke 10:19).

Don't let the devil overtake you!

THE DIVISIONS OF SATAN'S ARMY

Next, we are to take from the strong man *"all his armor in which he trusted"* (Luke 11:23). What is the devil armed with? Ephesians 6: 12 tells us: *"We wrestle not against flesh and blood, but against principalities, against powers, against the rulers of the darkness of this world, against spiritual wickedness in high places."*

In this one verse we find the five divisions of Satan's army:

Division #1: Demon Spirits

This scripture tells us that *"we wrestle not against flesh and blood."* We are at war with the devil and his agents. Demons could number in the billions.

Division #2: Principalities

"Principalities" comes from the Greek word "archas"— the chief rulers of the highest rank and order in Satan's kingdom. Thank God, there is One even higher than Satan: the Lord Jesus Himself, *"and ye are complete in him, which is the head of all principality and power"* (Colossians 2:10).

Division #3: Powers

Powers denotes the authorities operating under Satan's chief rulers, who are executing their will. One translation calls them "sergeants."

Division #4: Rulers of the Darkness of this World

"World" here comes from *cosmos,* the world's system. And these rulers are men who are yielded to the power of Satan. I believe Herod was one such man, and Hitler was another.

Division #5: Spiritual Wickedness in High Places

This includes wicked spirits in the heavenlies, fallen angels, and evil princes who lead nations and atmospheres. The prince of Persia, mentioned in the book of Daniel, was one of them.

WHAT ABOUT GOD'S ARMY?

I believe the reason Paul mentioned demons first is because when we encounter the demonic realm, that is our initial contact. So when Jesus said a strong man is *"fully armed"* (Luke 11:22), he has a well-organized army.

It is interesting that Satan copied God, because God Almighty has five divisions in His heavenly army: (1) seraphim, (2) cherubim, (3) living creatures, (4) archangels, and (5) common angels.

The heavenly order begins with a seraph, the one who

introduces and presents the glory of God. We come to the glory before becoming acquainted with the angelic hosts.

What a contrast that is! When we encounter Satan we are dealing with demons. But when we encounter angels we first deal with the glory of God.

We enter into glory through thanksgiving, praise, and worship, which releases the angelic realm. That is why praise and worship is the door to victory.

We can defeat Satan because we come against him from a higher plateau.

Remember, Jesus said, *"When a stronger than he [Satan] comes upon him and overcomes him"* (Luke 11:23). We are standing in heavenly places, with Christ, far above all powers. We come at the devil from above, not below. That is how you overpower the enemy.

FREE THE CAPTIVES!

The stronger man—that's you—not only takes away the devil's armor, but *"divides his spoils"* (Luke 11:23).

The spoils are the former victories Satan has had against us. You don't take spoils unless you have won a battle, and since the devil has had certain triumphs, his spoils have also become weapons against us.

The devil's spoils include the captives he has been holding. So when you divide the spoil, you drive away demons and the devil's wicked rulers, and release the prisoners Satan has kept all this time. Not only are you driving the powers of hell away, you are breaking chains, opening doors, and letting the captives go free.

In our crusades when I lead the crowds in praise and

worship, chains begin to fall, devils begin to flee, and sickness begins to depart. Satan himself runs like a coward, and his army scatters with him!

It is a fulfillment of the amazing statement Jesus made: *"He that is not with me is against me; and he that gathereth not with me scattereth abroad"* (Matthew 12:30).

Who are we gathering? Those prisoners who have just been released. You are bringing the souls of men and women to the cross.

YOUR EQUIPMENT

All twelve of the demonic spirits we detailed in the last chapter must be overcome and disarmed. However, before that can happen, we must make sure we are equipped and ready.

We begin by making certain our prayer life is built on a solid foundation. The psalmist wrote: *"I will call upon the LORD, who is worthy to be praised: so shall I be saved from mine enemies"* (Psalm 18:3).

The enemies are the host of Satan—the devil and his camp. So only when we call on God will we be free from the devil. If we remain entangled in the bondage of Satan, how can we fight and defeat him? Jesus tells us, *"Verily I say unto you, Whatsoever ye shall bind on earth shall be bound in heaven: and whatsoever ye shall loose on earth shall be loosed in heaven"* (Matthew 18:18).

Your key to victory, however, is found in the verses that follow: *"Again I say unto you, that if two of you shall agree on earth as touching any thing that they shall ask, it shall be done for them of my Father which is in heaven. For where two or three are gathered together in my name, there am I in the midst of them"* (verses 19-20).

Binding Satan is not a task you are asked to accomplish by yourself. It requires unity! We fight the devil together.

When we study Matthew 18, we discover that before and after we are told to bind the devil, as believers we must be reconciled to one another. Back up to verses 15-17 and we find: *"If thy brother shall trespass against thee, go and tell him his fault between thee and him alone: if he shall hear thee, thou hast gained thy brother. But if he will not hear thee, then take with thee one or two more, that in the mouth of two or three witnesses every word may be established. And if he shall neglect to hear them, tell it unto the church: but if he neglect to hear the church, let him be unto thee as an heathen man and a publican."*

The Lord is talking about reconciliation, forgiveness, oneness, and unity. Then, immediately, He speaks of binding Satan.

What is the message? None of us can conquer the strong man alone. It requires unity, being in one accord. *"Again I say to you"*—Jesus is saying that in order to accomplish what He just told us, it is essential that we be united in fellowship with the saints. He continues, *"If two of you shall agree on earth as touching anything that they shall ask"* (verse 29). What do we ask and pray for? Binding the enemy. And when we do, the Lord promises to be right there with us.

Never forget that the One who is binding the devil is the Lord. As we come together in oneness, the Lord's power and His Person are present.

The remaining portion of Matthew 18 is a lesson on forgiveness. It is impossible to harbor hate or malice in your heart and expect to have power against Satan. We are impotent against the devil if we are disconnected from the body of Christ! It takes unity to bind the forces of hell.

Jesus said, *"Ask, and it shall be given you; seek, and ye shall find; knock, and it shall be opened unto you"* (Luke 11:9, emphasis mine). There are certain things we ask for alone. For example, there is no need to be calling a friend for every prayer you want to pray. But if there is a strong man attacking your son or daughter, or a devil trying to destroy your family, it's time to find someone to agree with you in payer, to bind that spirit in Jesus' name. And the two of you must be one in the Spirit.

I was recently listening to a recorded message of Kathryn Kuhlman. She was warning against bringing anyone into a ministry who is not united with you in Spirit. She explained that you can meet someone who is born again, Spirit filled, and loves the Lord, but they just don't fit in unless their heart is joined with yours. When you agree, heaven responds.

Starting now, come against Satan's armies through prayer and being united with other believers; then you will destroy the devil's armor, free the captives, and gain major victories for both yourself and others.

CHAPTER 13

YOUR SECRET WEAPON

Istory books are filled with the dramatic accounts of decisive battles—Joshua conquering Jericho, the fall of Constantinople, the U.S. Civil War, Israel's Six-Day War, the invasion of Iraq, and hundreds of other earthshaking clashes.

Even though many choose to ignore the fact, there is a colossal conflict being waged at this very moment, with far more serious consequences than any battle ever recorded. This is the one between God's children and Satan.

In this eternal conflict, you and I have a secret weapon to use against the enemy—the mighty Word of God. In this chapter I want to show you why it is the only artillery you need to totally defeat Satan.

Today, I see many Christians crouching in a defensive position, hiding behind a barrier or running away from the devil. That is not the way it's supposed to be. God longs for us to become a powerful, effective force, destroying the power of Satan. The Lord is not looking for an army hunkered down behind a bush singing, "There is power, power, wonder working power, in the blood of the Lamb." Instead, God wants us on the front line, demolishing the enemy. When Satan makes an appearance, we are to rise up and defeat his purpose.

Jesus stated this awesome truth: *"I will build my church; and the gates of hell shall not prevail against it"* (Matthew 16:18). The term *"gates of hell"* refers to the power or the authority of Satan, and according to the Bible, God's plan will not be stopped.

This is not a picture of the enemy's forces targeting you. Just the opposite, you are going against hell itself. You are opposing and preventing its actions.

Scripture proclaims, *"Thanks be unto God, which always causeth us to triumph in Christ, and maketh manifest the savour [aroma] of his knowledge by us in every place"* (2 Corinthians 2:14).

START CELEBRATING

A triumph is not winning a victory, rather the *celebration* of a victory. And never overlook the word *always*. It is not about defeating the devil just once, but forever.

In truth, God has called us to enforce the victory of Calvary over the enemy and rejoice in a work that is finished. We celebrate that triumph in the power of the Holy Spirit with authority and faith in His mighty name. Scripture confirms: *"This is the victory that overcometh the world, even our faith"* (1 John 5:4).

Triumph is the result of our total dependence and trust in the Lord. It has nothing to do with placing our faith in faith. We hold to His promises and glory in what was accomplished at the cross, because God *"giveth us the victory through our Lord Jesus Christ"* (1 Corinthians 15:57). Apart from Christ there is no eternal life, victory, or conquest over Satan.

VICTORY THROUGH OBEDIENCE

In this battle *"the weapons of our warfare are not carnal, but mighty through God to the pulling down of strongholds; casting down imaginations, and every high thing that exalteth itself against the knowledge of God, and bringing into captivity every thought to the obedience of Christ"* (2 Corinthians 10:4-5).

As a result, any area of our life where Satan has a stronghold can be conquered. However, if we take a close look at this passage, it tells us exactly how strongholds can be conquered. The process begins by *"casting down imaginations,"* getting rid of mental images and arguments that are not based on truth.

To fully understand the implication of the passage above, we need to read the next verse: *"Having in a readiness to revenge all disobedience, when your obedience is fulfilled"* (verse 6).

What a revelation! This tells us that when we begin to obey the Lord, everything that opposes Him (all disobedience) will be silenced. It will not touch our families, homes, or loved ones. God will begin to work on our behalf!

IT'S ALL OR NOTHING

The Lord does not approve of partial victories. It's all or nothing! The psalmist details a conquest that is definite, total, and permanent:

It is God who arms me with strength, and makes my way perfect. He makes my feet like the feet of deer, and sets me on my high places. He teaches my hands to make war, so that my arms can bend a bow of bronze. You have also given me the shield of Your salvation; Your right hand has held me up, Your gentleness has made me great.

You enlarged my path under me, so my feet did not slip. I have pursued my enemies and overtaken them; neither did I turn back again till they were destroyed. I have wounded them, so that they could not rise; they have fallen under my feet. For You have armed me with strength for the battle; You have subdued under me those who rose up against me.

You have also given me the necks of my enemies, so that I destroyed those who hated me. They cried out, but there was none to save; even to the LORD, but He did not answer them. Then I beat them as fine as the dust before the wind; I cast them out like dirt in the streets (Psalm 18:32-42, NKJV).

When your adversaries are beaten down until they are nothing but dust in the air, that is total victory!

We are not commanded to fight just 30 percent of the battle, or even 60. Our Commander-in-Chief demands a 100 percent effort. There is no time to pull back and complain, "Well, I've had it." You never give in until the enemy is totally subdued.

It's time to recognize Satan for who he is—a coward, not a champion.

NEVER RETREAT

There's a lesson to be learned in the account of Joshua's second invasion of the city of Ai. You may recall that on his first attempt, Israel suffered a great loss because a soldier disobeyed God's command and plundered what was cursed during the battle of Jericho (Joshua 7). Because of that the Lord taught the children of Israel a lesson.

This time it was different. As the battle commenced, God told Joshua to do something quite unusual. He said, *"Stretch out the spear that is in thy hand toward Ai; for I will give it into thine hand. And Joshua stretched out the spear that he had in his hand toward the city"* (Joshua 8:18).

This chosen leader of God didn't throw the spear, he just held it in the air, even while his armies invaded the city: *"Joshua drew not his hand back, wherewith he stretched out the spear, until he [the armies of Israel] had utterly destroyed all the inhabitants of Ai"* (verse 26).

This amazing battle is symbolic of the struggle against Satan we are in today; one that will continue until every enemy is vanquished. Regardless of the obstacles, we must never retreat until the battle is won.

USE ALL YOUR ARROWS

If you lack faith and are willing to accept only a partial victory, the demons will harass you with thorns in your flesh. That's why you must keep the weapons of your warfare in your hand and never give up. Whether God offers you a spear, a rock, or an arrow, don't make a move until He gives the signal. And when He does, never deviate from the plan.

Once, as the prophet Elisha was suffering with an illness from which he would soon die, Joash, the king of Israel paid him a visit. Upon seeing him, the king cried openly, *"O my father, my father, the chariot of Israel"* (2 Kings 13:14).

Rather than thanking him for his care and concern, Elisha's first words were to ask the king to bring him a bow and arrows. The king obliged, and the prophet instructed him, *"Put thine hand upon the bow"* (verse 16). When he did, Elisha placed his feeble hand over the king's hand.

Then the prophet told him to open the window eastward and shoot. The king did what was requested; then Elisha uttered this prophetic word: *"The arrow of the LORD'S deliverance and the arrow of deliverance from Syria; for you must strike the Syrians...till you have destroyed them"* (verse 17, NKJV).

Next, Elisha told the king to take the remaining arrows and aim them at the ground, so *"he struck three times, and stopped"* (verse 18).

At that point, the prophet became angry with him and said, *"You should have struck five or six times; then you would have struck Syria till you had destroyed it! But now you will strike Syria only three times"* (verse 19).

With these words, Elisha was chastising him and in effect saying, "Why did you stop at three? You now will only have a 50 percent success in your battle with Syria."

Elisha died, but his prophecy lived on and proved to be correct.

THE DEVIL'S NUMBER ONE WEAPON

When we are facing any conflict in our lives, the Lord wants us to know that we can't leave the battlefield until the enemy is defeated. We must stay on our knees, keep declaring the promises of God, and never grow disheartened or quit until we have victory.

If you have children or loved ones who aren't living for the Lord and you want to see them brought into the Lord's kingdom, you can't be lazy and delay calling on God. If you do, you've just lost the battle!

Do you know the devil's tactics? He doesn't attack with arrows in the natural realm. Instead, the enemy's weapons are his words. Remember, he told Eve in the Garden of Eden, *"Ye shall not surely die"* (Genesis 3:4).

Yes, the devil uses his voice. As the psalmist prayed, *"Attend unto me, and hear me: I mourn in my complaint, and make a noise; because of the voice of the enemy, because of the oppression of the wicked: for they cast iniquity upon me, and in wrath they hate me"* (Psalm 55:2-3).

Demons speak against Christians every single day. At this very moment, in the kingdom of Satan, witches pronounce curses over believers. A former member of the occult who is now a Christian once told me, "In our gatherings we would speak against you and your ministry."

In the psalm above, David was praying, "I don't know what's going on in my life, I'm being bombarded by the words of demons. It's as if there is a curse upon me. I can feel their anger."

He continued, *"My heart is sore pained within me: and the terrors of death are fallen upon me. Fearfulness and trembling are come upon me, and horror hath overwhelmed me. And I said, Oh that I had wings like a dove! for then would I fly away, and be at rest. Lo, then would I wander far off, and remain in the wilderness. I would hasten my escape from the windy storm and tempest"* (verses 4-8).

He wanted to run away from this torment, and he was looking for help from heaven.

HIGH PRAISES

Have you ever been in a situation where you felt such

mental anguish that you looked for a way of escape? Let me share a scripture that will save your life: *"By the word of Your lips, I have kept away from the paths of the destroyer"* (Psalm 17:4, NKJV).

Your deliverance and protection are the result of listening to and speaking the Word of God. It will keep you from walking down the dead-end, disastrous roads of the enemy.

If you are a born again believer, the Lord has a word especially for you: *"Let the saints be joyful in glory: let them sing aloud upon their beds. Let the high praises of God be in their mouth, and a two-edged sword in their hand"* (Psalm 149:5-6).

Why the singing and praising? These are powerful weapons against the enemy. *"To execute vengeance upon the heathen, and punishments upon the people; to bind their kings with chains, and their nobles with fetters of iron; to execute upon them the judgment written: this honour have all his saints"* (verses 7-9).

These verses speak directly to the principalities and power of Satan. It is why you can confidently claim this promise of God: *"No weapon that is formed against thee shall prosper; and every tongue that shall rise against thee in judgment thou shalt condemn"* (Isaiah 54:17).

The tongue that is against you belongs to the devil. You are attacked because words are directed at you from the demonic realm. To protect yourself you must speak Scripture. When you do, you bring judgment and destruction to the kingdom of hell.

Keep praying, and keep speaking the Word of God until the enemy becomes as dust. Then you will be able to declare, *"When I cry unto thee, then shall mine enemies turn back: this I know; for God is for me"* (Psalm 56:9).

Praise the Lord!

IT IS WRITTEN

When Jesus was baptized by John in the Jordan River, suddenly the heavens opened and the voice of God spoke, *"This is my beloved Son, in whom I am well pleased"* (Matthew 3:17).

"My Son!" The angels heard it, the world heard it, and Satan heard it. Even more, the Holy Spirit confirmed it by coming to rest upon the Son of God in the form of a dove.

It was only a few days later that Jesus was in the wilderness being tempted by the devil—the same devil who heard the voice of the Almighty. That is why Satan jeered, *"If thou be the Son of God, command this stone that it be made bread"* (Luke 4:3).

Jesus had every right to respond, "Didn't you hear God say who I am? Why are you questioning Him?" But the Lord didn't even mention the experience at the Jordan. Instead, Jesus used the Holy Word of God to counterattack Satan when He said, *"It is written, That man shall not live by bread alone, but by every word of God"* (verse 5).

That is significant! I can't count the number of times I have heard people say, "God spoke to me!" Your weapon that will defeat the enemy, however, is not what you hear, nor your experiences with the Lord, but the written Word of God.

There is no word or additional revelation beyond the Word of God.

THE WORD OF YOUR TESTIMONY

We often hear people refer to being an "overcomer." This

is certainly a goal worth striving for, but how do we reach such a place? There is only one way. In Revelation 12:11, we read, *"They overcame him by the blood of the Lamb, and by the word of their testimony."*

If you are unsure who is spoken of as "him," look at the previous verse. It is Satan himself, *"the accuser of the brethren is cast down"* (verse 10), And the "brethren" are you and me, the church. This means we defeat Satan by the blood that was shed on the cross and the words we launch from our lips.

At the end of verse 11 we read this sobering statement: *"They loved not their lives unto the death."* They were willing to pay the ultimate price for what they believed. To put it bluntly, what you say may cost you your life!

All through His ministry, when Jesus spoke there was destruction in the kingdom of hell. He cast out demons with the words that flowed from His mouth!

The Lord prophesied that after He returned to heaven the believers on earth would do even greater things than He had accomplished (John 14:12). All this is possible because of the power God has placed in the mouths of those who believe in Him.

I am not talking about naming and claiming a new car or a diamond ring. It's not what we desire, but what the Word of God declares. To become an overcomer, make sure your objective is accompanied by "Thus saith the Lord."

The only way to defeat Satan is to have the Word *abiding* in you: *"I have written unto you, fathers, because ye have known him that is from the beginning. I have written unto you, young men, because ye are strong, and the word of God abideth in you, and ye have overcome the wicked one"* (1 John 2:14).

WAKE UP!

We must learn to attune our ears to God when He asks, "Why are you fearful of the devil?"

The Almighty wants to know, *"Who are you that you should be afraid?...you forget the LORD your Maker, Who stretched out the heavens and laid the foundations of the earth; you have feared continually every day because of the fury of the oppressor, when he has prepared to destroy. And where is the fury of the oppressor?"* (Isaiah 51:12-13, NKJV).

Here, God directly challenged the devil, as if to say, "I dare you to be angry when I show up!" And the Lord is telling us to stop trembling in our boots over the enemy. Wake up!

Start relying on and trusting in God. Fear God instead of the devil.

Then the Lord painted this picture: *"The captive exile hastens, that he may be loosed, that he should not die in the pit, and that his bread should not fail"* (verse 14).

God was looking at a man who was bound by the devil, worried that he would die of hunger and wanting to be free from the trap in which he found himself.

Next, the Lord God Almighty made an appearance, proclaiming, *"I am the LORD your God, Who divided the sea whose waves roared"* (verse 15).

No matter what situation you find yourself in, the Lord is all-sufficient. He is all you need. God can bring peace to any storm or situation.

Finally, God made this amazing statement. *"I have put my words in thy mouth"* (verse 16). This is your key to victory! He places His anointed Word inside you, and when you declare it with your lips and believe it in your heart, whatever binds you will be loosed.

Oh, the miraculous power of His Word.

Now the Lord can begin working through you. *"I have covered you with the shadow of My hand, that I may plant the heavens, lay the foundations of the earth, and say to Zion, 'You are My people'"* (verse 16).

What an awesome truth! When you begin speaking the Word, God *works* the Word. The planting has begun, and a great harvest is being prepared.

LET IT SHINE!

The Word in your mouth will turn night into day. The psalmist looked up to heaven and said, *"Thou wilt light my candle: the LORD my God will enlighten my darkness* (Psalm 18:28).

How does this happen? By your words: *"Thou shalt also decree a thing, and it shall be established unto thee: and the light shall shine upon thy ways"* (Job 22:28).

Wow! Your path will be illuminated when you speak the Word. Yes, the Word is a lamp unto your feet, but the light is turned on when the Word is released from your mouth.

YOUR GUARANTEE

Any authority you may acquire on earth depends on the person who grants it. For example, you can walk into a bank and try to falsely sign my name on a check. You will either be sued or spend time behind bars. But if I give you instructions and legally sign my name to the request, you have my backing 100 percent!

The Lord Jesus is no different. He said, *"Whatsoever ye shall ask in my name, that will I do, that the Father may be glorified in the Son"* (John 14:13). When we walk in His authority, He guarantees results.

The opposite is also true. If you steal the Lord's name without His permission, woe unto you!

When the apostle Paul was preaching at Ephesus, his ministry was accompanied by mighty miracles. The Bible tells how some vagabond Jews who were exorcists tried to imitate Paul. They took it upon themselves, *"to call over them which had evil spirits the name of the LORD Jesus, saying, We adjure you by Jesus whom Paul preacheth"* (Acts 19:13). When they tried this on a possessed man, the evil spirit answered, *"Jesus I know, and Paul I know; but who are ye?"* (verse 15).

The tormented individual jumped on these imposters, overcame them, and ran them out of town. As a result, the name of Jesus was magnified: *"Also, many of those who had practiced magic brought their books together and burned them in the sight of all"* (verse 19, NKJV).

It is the name of Jesus and the power of God's Word that gives us authority over the enemy.

BREAK THE CHAINS

Jesus conquered and defeated Satan for you and me. He announced to mankind, *"The Spirit of the Lord is upon me, because he hath anointed me to preach the gospel to the poor; he hath sent me to heal the brokenhearted, to preach deliverance to the captives, and recovering of sight to the blind, to set at liberty them that are bruised"* (Luke 4:18).

Since that is true, why are some Christians still shackled by Satan? The prison door has been opened, yet they remain captive. We don't have to break the chains, they have already been broken. But it is up to you and me to walk into God's freedom.

That reminds me of the story about training an elephant. When this elephant was still a baby, its trainer chained one of its legs securely to a post imbedded in the ground. Of course, the young elephant resisted and tried to pull away but couldn't.

As the animal grew larger, it became stronger than the chain yet never knew it. Why? Because his limited boundaries had been imprinted on his brain as a baby. Even though this huge adult animal was far stronger than the chain, in its mind it was still bound.

There are many believers caught in this same mental trap. Through God they are stronger than the devil, but they aren't aware of it. They have not yet experienced the power of God and remain imprisoned by their fear and weakness. If only they knew that *"for this purpose the Son of God was manifested, that he might destroy the works of the devil"* (1 John 3:8).

On the cross of Calvary, Jesus uttered, *"It is finished"* (John 19:30).

At that moment, what He came to accomplish was completed. Satan was conquered, and by accepting His work by faith, we are gloriously set free.

IT'S BEEN CONQUERED

Remember, even before Joshua crossed the Jordan River and entered the Promised Land, the Lord had told him, *"Every place that the sole of your foot will tread upon I have given you"* (Joshua 1:3, NKJV). The territory had already been conquered; all Joshua and the children of Israel had to do was walk in and possess it.

The door to their possession, however, was to declare the Word of the Lord. God said to Joshua, *"This Book of the Law shall not depart from your mouth, but you shall meditate in it day and night, that you may observe to do according to all that is written in it. For then you will make your way prosperous, and then you will have good success"* (verse 8).

If you will listen, God has the same message for you. Jesus promises, *"I will give unto thee the keys of the kingdom of heaven"* (Matthew 16:19). He has already overcome the devil and is telling you to walk out of your prison and possess the land.

You are the devil's master! He has to obey you.

Unfortunately, demons are like dogs—they know when their owners are scared. They can sense your fear. As a result, if we fail to exert our authority, they will take total control over us and cause havoc.

The devil sees us as we see ourselves. That is why we must believe God's Word and know who we are in Him before we can step onto the battlefield against the forces of hell. This is a life-changing truth.

When Moses sent out the twelve spies to scout out the Promised Land—one from each of the tribes of Israel—ten returned with negative reports. Yes, Canaan was flowing with milk and honey, but they were absolutely terrified of the giants in the land: *"There we saw the giants...and we were like grasshoppers in our own sight, and so we were in their sight"* (Numbers 13:33).

Whether it is strength or weakness, the vision you have of yourself is exactly how Satan perceives you. That is why your self-image must be based on God's Word and what He says about your present and your future. You are the head and not the tail (Deuteronomy 28:13). You are more than a conqueror (Romans 8:37). When you believe God's Word, nothing is impossible to you (Mark 9:23).

WATCH WHAT YOU SAY!

There comes a time when the Lord says, "If you are ignoring My Word, fine. I'll just go ahead and do whatever I hear you talk about. I will leave you to your own desires."

For example, God promised the children of Israel that He would lead them to the Promised Land, but on the journey they were complaining about dying in the desert. They murmured, *"Would it not be better for us to return to Egypt?"* (Numbers 14:3).

God does what He hears us talk about: *"As truly as I live, saith the LORD, as ye have spoken in mine ears, so will I do to you"* (Numbers 14:28).

Since disaster was what the children of Israel spoke of, that's what they were going to receive: God declared, *"The carcasses of you who have complained against Me shall fall in this wilderness"* (verse 29). And that's exactly what happened (verse 36).

HOW THE WORD COMES ALIVE

How committed are you to reading and studying the Bible—including all the genealogies, the laws, the prophets, the Gospels, the epistles, and more? If you don't understand each word, that's all right. Read and re-read every chapter and verse until you do. In the process, the scripture will spring up and become alive in your heart.

I can't begin to express how excited I was when I first discovered that a portion of text in Genesis is explained in Isaiah, and a section of Ezekiel is only understood in

Ephesians, and some verses in Exodus are revealed in Revelation. You will learn that the Bible interprets itself.

As you read the Word, there will be questions, but don't try to find the answers overnight. Keep reading, because what seems like a problem in one book will be solved in another. Like a puzzle, it all fits together until you have the entire, clear picture.

Read. Study. Pray. Then read some more. God tells us, *"My people are destroyed for lack of knowledge"* (Hosea 4:6). We are to *"walk worthy of the Lord...being fruitful in every good work, and increasing in the knowledge of God"* (Colossians 1:10).

THE ONLY WEAPON YOU NEED

If you want to know the mind and the will of the Lord, read what He wrote. Don't keep searching for modern-day prophets to say, "Well, God is saying this to me."

The gift of prophecy is for edification, exhortation, and comfort. It is not your weapon. Even the wonderful gifts of wisdom, knowledge, faith, and the working of miracles are not your artillery against Satan. In this war, you only need one weapon—the written Word of God. When we mix the Word of God with fervent prayer we have a sharp, two-edged sword.

The problem we face is that most people don't know what is written! They're not reading what God has said, and as a result, the devil makes a mess out of their lives. If we don't know Scripture, how can we fight Satan? The Scripture states that God watches over His Word to perform it.

The Bible declares that you will exercise authority over the enemy when the Word is in you: *"Then the LORD put forth*

His hand and touched my mouth, and the LORD said to me: 'Behold, I have put My words in your mouth. See, I have this day set you over the nations and over the kingdoms, to root out and to pull down, to destroy and to throw down, to build and to plant'" (Jeremiah 1:9-10, NKJV).

You will experience God's promises.

TRUE DELIVERANCE

God tells us we can choose our own master. We can either obey the Lord or the devil. Whoever you yield yourself to will be your master. Scripture tells us, *"Do you not know that to whom you present yourselves slaves to obey, you are that one's slaves whom you obey, whether of sin leading to death, or of obedience leading to righteousness?"* (Romans 6:16, NKJV).

You say, "Well, I'm delivered from the devil." No, you are only free if you hear and obey God's Word. Remember, Israel was brought out of Egypt, but they lost their deliverance through disobedience.

Scripture tells us what will happen to those who refuse to follow God's Word and His ways: *"All you beasts of the field, come to devour, all you beasts in the forest"* (Isaiah 56:9, NKJV). Why is there devouring? Why are people in bondage? Why are they losing what God wants them to have? *"His watchmen are blind, they are all ignorant; they are all dumb dogs, they cannot bark; sleeping, lying down, loving to slumber. Yes, they are greedy dogs which never have enough. And they are shepherds who cannot understand; they all look to their own way, every one for his own gain, from his own territory"* (verses 10-11).

These people weren't serious about obeying God's Word.

They just wanted to have a good time. One says, *"Come...I will bring wine, and we will fill ourselves with intoxicating drink; tomorrow will be as today, and much more abundant"* (verse 12).

Sadly, this describes many so-called churches today. They operate like social clubs that would rather have fun than offend anybody. Instead of preaching the Word, they talk about what people want to hear. This was prophesied by the apostle Paul: *"The time will come when they will not endure sound doctrine; but after their own lusts shall they heap to themselves teachers, having itching ears. And they shall turn away their ears from the truth, and shall be turned unto fables"* (2 Timothy 4:3-4).

God calls these people "blind," "ignorant," and "dumb dogs." They are demon oppressed. They don't recognize truth or know where to turn for real help. They are being told how to deal with their emotions, when their emotions are troubled by devils.

It is a mirror image of what was spoken of by Peter: *"While they promise them liberty, they themselves are the servants of corruption: for of whom a man is overcome, of the same is he brought in bondage"* (2 Peter 2:19).

Whatever sin or problem overcomes you will bind you. That is why we are commanded, *"Love not the world, neither the things that are in the world. If any man love the world, the love of the Father is not in him"* (1 John 2:15).

Let Christ be the Lord and Master of your life.

Take Charge!

Start claiming victory in Jesus' name, for you are a follower of the Victor Himself! God has *"delivered us from the power*

189

of darkness, and hath translated us into the kingdom of his dear Son" (Colossians 1:13).

If you have been liberated from the clutches of the devil, it's worth shouting about! *"Let the redeemed of the LORD say so"* (Psalm 107:2).

Not only do we have redemption through the blood of Jesus, but *"the forgiveness of sins"* (Colossians 1:14).

You are *"complete in him, which is the head of all principality and power"* (Colossians 2:10). As a result, you are joined to the One who is Lord of all: *"Having disarmed principalities and powers, He made a public spectacle of them, triumphing over them in it"* (verse 15, NKJV).

When the Lord rose from the dead, He left an eternally defeated Satan behind. He wasn't talking about sometime in the future. The work is finished!

You can become a master over the devil overnight if you will only believe God's Word. Jesus declares, *"Behold, I give unto you power [authority] to tread on serpents and scorpions, and over all the power of the enemy: and nothing shall by any means hurt you"* (Luke 10:19).

What a mighty promise!

The men and women who are harmed by the devil are the ones who don't act on this scripture. If you are intimidated, you will be attacked and defeated.

BE A BOLD BELIEVER

The virtues of boldness and righteousness go hand in hand: *"The righteous are bold as a lion"* (Proverbs 28:1).

After the Upper Room experience on the Day of Pentecost, Peter and John began to proclaim the message of Christ. The Bible records, *"When they saw the boldness of*

Peter and John, and perceived that they were uneducated and untrained men, they marveled. And they realized that they had been with Jesus" (Acts 4:13).

Miracles were taking place left and right and thousands were being saved. At the gate of the temple, Peter said to a beggar who had been lame from birth, *"Silver and gold I have none; but such as I have give I thee: In the name of Jesus Christ of Nazareth rise up and walk"* (Acts 3:6).

Peter took him by his hand, lifted him up, and immediately his feet and ankle bones received strength. The man stood up and entered the temple with Peter and John, *"walking, and leaping, and praising God"* (verse 8).

The news of this dramatic healing spread like wildfire and the religious leaders were greatly disturbed and had the apostles arrested. They tried to silence these followers of Christ with threats, but Peter and John spoke back to them, saying, *"Whether it is right in the sight of God to listen to you more than to God, you judge. For we cannot but speak the things which we have seen and heard"* (verses 19-20, NKJV).

As soon as Peter and John were released, they met with fellow believers who were praising the Lord, and *"the place where they were assembled together was shaken; and they were all filled with the Holy Spirit, and they spoke the word of God with boldness"* (verse 31).

They had absolutely no fear of what man might say!

If you ever run into a person who claims he is righteous, yet is afraid of the devil, he is headed for danger, because Scripture warns, *"The fearful, and unbelieving...shall have their part in the lake which burneth with fire and brimstone"* (Revelation 21:8).

The consequences of fear are eternal.

DESTROY THE DEVIL!

Instead of being a coward, head in the direction of the enemy and start speaking the Word of God. Then watch how the Lord reacts: *"He will thrust out the enemy from before you, and will say, 'Destroy!'"* (Deuteronomy 33:27, NKJV).

In that same verse, we are assured that while we are assaulting the enemy *"the eternal God is your refuge, and underneath are the everlasting arms"* (verse 27).

The Lord has your back as you launch an all-out attack against Satan. Your faith and obedience to God's Word places fear in the heart of demons.

During an Old Testament battle, five kings fled into hiding when Joshua's armies appeared. Later, when they were found cowering in a cave and brought before Joshua, he told his captains, *"Come near, put your feet on the necks of these kings"* (Joshua 10:24, NKJV). When they did, Joshua assured his men, *"Do not be afraid, nor be dismayed; be strong and of good courage, for thus the LORD will do to all your enemies against whom you fight"* (verse 25).

Praise God! The devil is under your foot!

Let us recap our battle plan: Love the Lord, stand on His Word, and let God do the rest. Remember, we are a majority when God Almighty is on our side. *"One [shall] chase a thousand, and two put ten thousand to flight"* (Deuteronomy 32:30).

The war still rages and the battle is intense, but you will totally defeat the devil by using your powerful secret weapon—the mighty Word of God!

PART III

THE
FINAL BATTLE

CHAPTER 14

GOD'S END-TIME AGENDA

Now will the conflict between angels and demons end? What is next on God's schedule? What about the Rapture, the Tribulation, the Millennium, the second coming of Christ, and the final battle?

Let's take them one at a time.

THE REALITY OF THE RAPTURE

The most startling event in history is about to take place: the rapture of the church. Suddenly millions of Christians, both dead and alive, will be caught up to meet the Lord in the air. As the apostle Paul wrote, *"I would not have you to be ignorant, brethren, concerning them which are asleep, that ye sorrow not, even as others which have no hope. For if we believe that Jesus died and rose again, even so them also which sleep in Jesus will God bring with him"* (1 Thessalonians 4:13-14).

Who are the ones who are asleep? They are believers in Christ who have already passed from this life: *"This we say unto you by the word of the Lord, that we which are alive and remain unto the coming of the Lord shall not prevent them which are asleep"* (verse 15). When Paul said, *"by the word of the Lord,"* we know this is not the apostles's own idea; it was given to him by God. *"The Lord himself shall descend from heaven with a shout, with the voice of the archangel, and with the trump of God"* (verse 16). The archangel here is Gabriel, who has always been involved in major divine announcements.

We are told that *"the dead in Christ shall rise first: then we which are alive and remain shall be caught up together with them in the clouds, to meet the Lord in the air"* (verses 16-17).

In the early questions arose concerning the resurrection of the dead. Paul addressed this matter with the believers at Corinth: *"Now if Christ be preached that he rose from the dead, how say some among you that there is no resurrection of the dead? But if there be no resurrection of the dead, then is Christ not risen: and if Christ be not risen, then is our preaching vain, and your faith is also vain. Yea, and we are found false witnesses of God; because we have testified of God that he raised up Christ"* (1 Corinthians 15:12-15).

Later Paul taught, *"Every man in his own order: Christ the firstfruits; afterward they that are Christ's at his coming. Then cometh the end, when he shall have delivered up the kingdom to God, even the Father; when he shall have put down all rule and all authority and power"* (verses 23-24).

This clearly states the Resurrection is a reality—and so is the Rapture: *"Behold, I tell you a mystery: We shall not all sleep, but we shall all be changed—in a moment, in the twinkling of an eye, at the last trumpet. For the trumpet will sound, and the dead will be raised incorruptible, and we shall be changed"* (verses 51-52, NKJV).

Paul described this as "a mystery" because it was a truth

that was hidden from the church. Centuries earlier, the prophet Isaiah wrote, *"Your dead shall live; together with my dead body they shall arise...And the earth shall cast out the dead"* (Isaiah 26:19, NKJV).

And the same power that raised Jesus from the grave will bring millions out of their tombs.

Concerning the Rapture, Paul tells us, *"For this corruptible must put on incorruption, and this mortal must put on immortality"* (1 Corinthians 15:53).

In John's revelation, the question was asked, *"Who are these arrayed in white robes, and where did they come from?"* (Revelation 7:13, NKJV). An elder in heaven answered, *"These are the ones who come out of [escaped] the great tribulation, and washed their robes and made them white in the blood of the Lamb"* (verse 14).

He saw you and me—the raptured church—in heaven. These were not angels, but blood-washed saints.

WILL GOD JUDGE SAINTS WITH SINNERS?

The Bible is emphatic that God Almighty will not allow the righteous to be judged with the wicked. When Abraham was interceding for those who were living right, he said to the Lord: *"Far be it from You to do such a thing as this, to slay the righteous with the wicked, so that the righteous should be as the wicked...Shall not the Judge of all the earth do right?"* (Genesis 18:25, NKJV).

He was concerned, telling God, "This is not Your nature. Surely, You are going to do the right thing."

Later, God proved that He would not punish the righteous with the sinner. Just before He rained down fire and brimstone on Sodom and Gomorrah, He sent an angel to warn Lot and his family: *"Hurry, escape there [to the city of Zoar]. For I cannot do anything until you arrive there"* (Genesis 19:22, NKJV).

The angel explained he could not do anything differently because he was under orders from God Almighty. If you read the story carefully, you discover that when Lot lingered, the angels physically *"took hold of his hand, his wife's hand, and the hands of his two daughters...and they brought him out and set him outside the city"* (verse 16). God told Lot that He would not destroy the city until he and his family were safe.

Since God will not judge the saints with the sinners, He will not allow His children to go through the Tribulation.

How can you be prepared for the Rapture? There is only one way: *"And now, little children, abide in him; that, when he shall appear, we may have confidence, and not be ashamed before him at his coming"* (1 John 2:28).

Some will be filled with remorse because they failed to obey the Lord's command: *"Occupy till I come"* (Luke 19:13).

THE NUMBER ONE SIGN

As I minister throughout the world, I am asked again and again, "How close are we to the Rapture?"

Without question, God uses Israel as a sign through whom He speaks to the church and to the nations. In fact, the angels of heaven and the demons of hell discover God's plans by watching what is taking place in Israel. It is a message that is unmistakable to the invisible world. When the demons see His plans, they oppose them, while the angels take action to see them accomplished.

Reading your Bible and getting to know the heart of God,

you will find He is committed to one people: Israel. As the church we are grafted into this historic land, partakers of the heavenly gift by grace. When God looks at the church, He sees only one tree, the children of Abraham.

The apostle Paul refers to us as *"the Israel of God"* (Galatians 6:16), but he is speaking of not only Jew but also Gentile. A promise that applies to Israel in the natural also applies to Israel in the spiritual, so both of us reap the benefits of the same promise. God does not have two brides; He only has one—Israel.

As followers of Christ, we are His people.

That does not dismiss the natural Jewish people from having an eternal plan. But what happens in the natural is God's voice to the spiritual. That is why Paul wrote, *"I am not ashamed of the gospel of Christ: for it is the power of God unto salvation to every one that believeth; to the Jew first, and also to the Greek"* (Romans 1:16).

A CRY FOR THE MESSIAH

Today, I am seeing a genuine openness among the Jewish people toward Christ that is unprecedented. It foreshadows God's dealings with spiritual Israel—His church.

The Bible says if the rejection of Christ by the Jews brought life to the Gentiles, how much greater it will be when they accept Him: *"If their being cast away is the reconciling of the world, what will their acceptance be but life from the dead?"* (Romans 11:15).

The same people who have scorned the message of the Gospel for the last 2,000 years are now beginning to slowly turn around and accept the truth. That tells me heaven has been moving upon the hearts of the Jews.

The day is drawing closer when Israel will cry for their Messiah with a far deeper hunger. I believe this will happen as a result of some devastating catastrophe. It could be a war, a major terror attack, or a new Holocaust.

Remember, the reason Joseph was revealed to his brothers was because of a famine in Egypt. Whether in the natural or the spiritual, some form of crisis will cause Israel to cry out, "Where is our Messiah?" As their cries echo louder, He will reveal Himself.

I don't believe it is mere coincidence that the song "Mhakim Lemashiah" ("Waiting for Messiah") by Jewish pop artist Shalom Hanoch has become one of the most popular songs in the history of Israeli music.

It tells me we are running out of time. As Jesus told His disciples, *"When they persecute you in this city, flee ye into another: for verily I say unto you, Ye shall not have gone over the cities of Israel, till the Son of man be come"* (Matthew 10:23).

In other words, we will not finish preaching the Gospel in Israel before Christ returns.

Israel is a small country the size of New Jersey, but there are many barriers to proclaiming the message of Christ in this land, including the opposition of the orthodox Jews.

AN ETERNAL PEOPLE

I believe God has extended His grace toward Israel because *"the Lord is not slack concerning his promise, as some men count slackness; but is longsuffering to us-ward, not willing that any should perish, but that all should come to repentance"* (2 Peter 3:9).

Our heavenly Father is patiently waiting until every man,

woman, and child has had the chance to hear the Gospel.

Before Israel accepts Christ, we will be raptured. How do I know this? It is written in God's Word: *"Blindness in part has happened to Israel until the fullness of the Gentiles has come in. And so all Israel will be saved, as it is written: 'The Deliverer will come out of Zion, and He will turn away ungodliness from Jacob; for this is My covenant with them, when I take away their sins'"* (Romans 11:25-27, NKJV).

At one point, the Lord Jesus stood on the Mount of Olives and cried over Jerusalem, saying, *"If you had known, even you, especially in this your day, the things that make for your peace! But now they are hidden from your eyes"* (Luke 19:42).

The Jews missed their hour of opportunity. Blindness fell on them and they have been under a veil for 2,000 years. God has allowed this to take place in order for the Gentiles to come into the kingdom.

When God gives the signal, the veil will be lifted. Instead of more Gentiles being saved, the Lord will turn His total attention back to His ancient beloved people.

Therefore, I believe we are in the last days for the plan of God to be fulfilled in this dispensation for the Gentiles. But we are on the brink of the beginning days for Israel.

There are no "last days" for the Jews. God will deal with them forever! They are eternal people with an eternal plan.

That is why I emphasize that if you watch Israel, you'll know God's next move.

It is noteworthy to observe how the Jewish nation has discovered that their only real friends in the world are evangelical Christians. Their leaders in Jerusalem have told this to me personally.

GET READY!

Every major move of God has begun with an angelic visitation:

- Before Abraham and Sarah had their promised son, angels arrived with the prophetic announcement (Genesis 18:1-16).
- Before Jacob received God's blessing, he wrestled with an angel (Genesis 32:24-32).
- Before Gideon defeated the Midianites with just a small army, an angel appeared to give him courage (Judges 6:11-23).
- Before Jesus was born, an angel visited Mary and foretold His birth (Luke 1:26-38).
- Before the Day of Pentecost, angels appeared to the apostles (Acts 1:10-11).
- In the great spiritual awakenings through the ages, angels have appeared before a mighty move of the Spirit.

Today, as I see what God is doing with His people, Israel, we are on the brink of a pre-rapture angelic visitation. God is about to send His messengers to earth to spark a mighty revival.

THE TRIBULATION AND CHRIST'S SECOND COMING

Immediately following the Rapture the seven-year tribulation period will begin.

During this time, no Gentiles will accept Christ as their Savior. Their opportunity for salvation will be over. The only people who will be saved during the Tribulation are the Jews.

Most Bible scholars believe this period will be divided into two parts. The first three and one half years is simply called "tribulation" (Revelation 6-10). The next three and one half years is "the great tribulation" (Revelation 13-19). The last season begins with the Antichrist invading Jerusalem, where wrath will befall him.

Following these seven years, the second coming of Christ will occur. The Lord will return visibly from heaven with the saints for the final war against the Antichrist. The apostle Paul tells us this evil ruler will be destroyed by the glory of the presence of God's Son: *"Then shall that Wicked be revealed, whom the Lord shall consume with the spirit of his mouth, and shall destroy with the brightness of his coming"* (2 Thessalonians 2:8).

This ushers in the millennial reign of Christ who will rule on earth for 1,000 years. Let's read what John describes in his revelation:

> *Then I saw an angel coming down from heaven, having the key to the bottomless pit and a great chain in his hand. He laid hold of the dragon, that serpent of old, who is the Devil and Satan, and bound him for a thousand years; and he cast him into the bottomless pit, and shut him up, and set a seal on him, so that he should deceive the nations no more till the thousand years were finished. But after these things he must be released for a little while.*
>
> *And I saw thrones, and they sat on them, and judgment was committed to them. Then I saw the souls of those who had been beheaded for their witness to Jesus and for the word of God, who had not*

worshiped the beast or his image, and had not received his mark on their foreheads or on their hands. And they lived and reigned with Christ for a thousand years. But the rest of the dead did not live again until the thousand years were finished. This is the first resurrection. Blessed and holy is he who has part in the first resurrection. Over such the second death has no power, but they shall be priests of God and of Christ, and shall reign with Him a thousand years" (Revelation 20:1-6, NKJV).

Once our Lord returns to the earth, there will still be people alive who have not made the Rapture or been killed in the wars during the Tribulation. We don't know how many that will number, but they will continue to live and multiply under the reign of the Messiah. We, the church, will reign with Him over them.

The Jewish people will continue to live in Israel during the Millennium, where Christ will have His throne. This will be an era of total peace, prosperity, and blessing. The sun will shine brighter, the days will be lengthened, and life on earth will be total paradise.

During the Millennium, God's plan will be different. We will reign with Christ and the Gospel will not be preached. The message of salvation is for our present season, for this dispensation of grace.

Here's the exciting part. Satan will be bound in the pit and no demons will be found on earth during Christ's thousand year reign. Sin will no longer be in control.

However, *"when the thousand years are expired, Satan shall be loosed out of his prison, and shall go out to deceive the nations which are in the four quarters of the earth"* (Revelation 20:7-8).

He will not deceive the church but the world. God will prove once and for all that the heart of man is wicked. Even after a thousand years of abundance and blessing, many will still turn against Him.

THE FINAL BATTLE

Satan may think he has gained a great victory, but his celebration will only be temporary. After misleading millions, he will convince them it is time for the final war against God and His people. From the nations of the world his evil armies will attack God's Holy City. Yet, when they arrive, fire will pour out of heaven and consume them. *"And the devil that deceived them was cast into the lake of fire and brimstone, where the beast and the false prophet are, and shall be tormented day and night for ever and ever"* (Revelation 20:10).

Finally, all who have ever lived will stand before God at the Great White Throne Judgment. The Book of Life will be opened and each man and woman will be judged by the way they lived: *"Whosoever was not found written in the book of life was cast into the lake of fire"* (verse 15). This is the second death.

For the believer, the story has an entirely different ending. John saw *"a new heaven and a new earth...the holy city, new Jerusalem, coming down from God out of heaven, prepared as a bride adorned for her husband"* (Revelation 21:1-2).

God will wipe away all tears from our eyes. There will be no more sorrow, crying, pain, or death (verse 4). Hallelujah!

What a glorious day that will be! *"There shall be no night there; and they need no candle, neither light of the sun; for the Lord God giveth them light: and they shall reign for ever and ever"* (Revelation 22:5).

MY PRAYER FOR YOU

If you have never asked Christ to be your Lord and Savior, let me share these four steps to salvation with you:

Step #1: Understand that God's desire for you is life, abundant and eternal.

Jesus declares, *"I am come that they might have life, and that they might have it more abundantly"* (John 10:10). This required the supreme sacrifice: *"For God so loved the world, that he gave his only begotten Son, that whosoever believeth in him should not perish, but have everlasting life"* (John 3:16).

Step #2: Realize that you are separated from God.

There is a gap between God and mankind that the Lord wants to fill, but people throughout the ages have made selfish choices to disobey God Almighty. The result is sin and death: *"There is a way which seemeth right unto a man, but the end thereof are the ways of death"* (Proverbs 14:12).

We know that *"the wages of sin is death; but the gift of God is eternal life through Jesus Christ our Lord"* (Romans 6:23).

Only God, through His Son, can fill man's emptiness.

Step #3: Accept the fact that God has provided only one solution to sin and separation from Himself.

Jesus Christ, His Son, is the only way to God. Only He can reconcile us to God the Father: *"God commendeth his love toward us, in that, while we were yet sinners, Christ died for us"* (Romans 5:8). *"For there is one God, and one mediator between God and men, the man Christ Jesus"* (1 Timothy 2:5).

Christ paid the penalty for our sin and rebellion against God by dying on the cross, shedding His blood, and rising from the dead to justify and reconcile you back to God the Father.

Step #4: Receive Jesus Christ as your Lord and Savior.

You can be brought back to God, and your relationship with Him can be restored by trusting in Christ alone to save your life from destruction. This happens when you ask Jesus Christ to take away your sin and to come into your heart to be your Lord and Savior.

God's Word is very clear: *"Behold, I stand at the door, and knock: if any man hear my voice, and open the door, I will come in to him, and will sup with him, and he with me"* (Revelation 3:20).

The Bible also declares, *"If thou shalt confess with thy mouth the Lord Jesus, and shalt believe in thine heart that God hath raised him from the dead, thou shalt be saved"* (Romans 10:9).

If you are willing to repent of your sins and receive Christ into your heart, please pray these words with me:

Dear Lord Jesus, I believe You are the Son of God. I believe You came to earth 2,000 years ago. I believe You died for me on the cross and shed Your blood for my salvation. I believe You rose from the dead and ascended on high. I believe You are coming back again to earth.

Dear Jesus, I am a sinner. Forgive my sin. Cleanse

me with Your precious blood. Come into my heart. Save my soul right now. I give You my life. I receive You as my Savior, my Lord, and my God. I am Yours forever, and I will serve and follow You the rest of my days. From this moment on, I belong to You only. I no longer belong to this world, nor to the enemy of my soul. I belong to You, and I am born again.
Amen!

Hallelujah! Your name is now written in the Book of Life and for eternity we will rejoice with the angels around the throne of God!

BENNY HINN MINISTRIES
P.O. BOX 162000
IRVING, TX 75016-2000

PHONE: 800-433-1900
INTERNET: www.bennyhinn.org